# *A Channel of Peace*

## *The Story of the Corrymeela Community*

3 /383258

*Ray Davey*

MarshallPickering
*An Imprint of* HarperCollins*Publishers*

Marshall Pickering is an Imprint of
HarperCollins*Religious*
Part of HarperCollins*Publishers*
77–85 Fulham Palace Road, London W6 8JB

First published in Great Britain
in 1993 by Marshall Pickering

1   3   5   7   9   10   8   6   4   2

A catalogue record for this book is
available from the British Library

ISBN 0 551 02797 5

Phototypeset by Harper Phototypesetters Limited,
Northampton, England
Printed and bound in Great Britain by
HarperCollinsManufacturing  Glasgow

Frank came to Ireland, after a brilliant career at Oxford to lecture in politics at Queen's University in Belfast. But he was never content to live in the safe seclusion of the class room. He set out to learn for himself what was really happening in the streets and ghettos. He fearlessly explored the troubled areas and patiently listened to the gut feelings of those who lived 'on the ground'. His work became not just a job but a mission. His students were challenged not to stop at analysis but to seek for solutions.

Eventually he came to Corrymeela. Almost immediately he felt at home in an atmosphere that accepted people on their own terms and as they are. He was a talented painter and soon he had started painting groups, not for the specialists but for anyone who was willing to try. He lavishly gave himself to discussing the political problems and possible solutions. Sometimes it would be with a group of sophisticated visitors from outside Ireland but more frequently with schools, Trade Unionists, political and social groups within Northern Ireland. His great patience and ability to listen and share his insights won him the respect and affection of multitudes from every background and tradition.

In turn Frank received much. For him the opportunity to meet with people of all classes and creeds was a constant source of renewal. At Corrymeela, the Christian gospel of reconciliation assumed the central importance it was to have for the rest of his life. One of his lasting legacies was with three other Corrymeela members, to set up the programme 'Understanding Conflict . . . and finding ways out of it'. This group seeks to integrate personal experience and academic learning and has already made a deep impact all over Ireland and beyond.

Last summer Frank took up the Chair of Peace and Co-operation Studies in Limerick. By that time, however, the first symptoms of his brain tumour were becoming obvious and he died on 10th February 1993.

*To Frank*

*What of our dearest friend,*
*A wraith, an empty shell?*
*That brilliant brain,*
*That all embracing smile*
*Snuffed out?*
*The paradox again.*
*What seems to us as dead,*
*Emancipated now*
*Can bondless roam*
*And enter hearts and minds*
*Unfettered, as in days of clay,*
*Fulfilling now*
*The task he'd just begun.*

# Contents

# *Preface*

Writing a book can be a solo activity or it can be shared with other people. The story falls into the latter category as I have relied on the insights and experience of so many others. This account describes the efforts of a large number of individuals who through the twenty-seven years have brought their energy, faith and hope to work together for new relationships in our divided society. My task was fulfilled mainly at the beginning in starting the journey. It resembles the role of the donkey-engine in the early days of railways, to prepare the way for the fuller operations that were to come.

So many have been part of the story. Some I have acknowledged in the text, but many others have been most helpful. Alan Evans and Alf McCreary have given me expert advice in style and presentation, Christine Smith (Publishing Manager of Marshall Pickering), could not have been more patient and encouraging through the long months of writing, John Morrow has read the script and made many valuable suggestions, Sister Deirdre of Thornhill College, Derry came to my assistance at a crucial time. Roger and Alison Curry have once again been a great support, especially when my morale was low. I am so pleased that Frank Wright had read and approved of part of the script and made useful comments before his untimely death. And my thanks go too to John Cole, former BBC Political Editor, for his Foreword.

Above all Kathleen has been an unending source of encouragement and invariably helped me through those frequent 'down periods'. Her accuracy in sorting out the script and her memory of people and events, in addition to her sensitivity, illustrated in the lines about Frank, have been invaluable and added much to the book.

14th April 1993

Ray Davey

# *Foreword*

## *By John Cole*

Corrymeela is the happier face of Northern Ireland. It 'shines like a good deed in a naughty world', as Portia said. After the horrors of the past quarter-century, this 'little candle' is desperately needed. It reminds the rest of the world of what those of us who grew up there have always known: that most of the people who live in Ulster are decent inheritors of an impossible political problem.

Ray Davey is the right man to tell this story, as he was the right man to be an inspiration of this beacon of decency almost thirty years ago. He learned his ecumenism as a wartime worker at the YMCA Centre in beleaguered Tobruk. He had it fortified by his years as a prisoner-of-war in Africa, Italy and Germany. As a young Presbyterian chaplain, he was allowed by the Germans to visit POW camps in the region of Dresden, just before the terrible air-raids of February 1945.

In those dreadful years, he learned the result of 'man's inhumanity to man'. He also learned, in the most personal way, that 'the enemy', close up, was just another part of the same tortured humanity, victim also of hatred and war. It was when Ray Davey returned to Belfast after the war, and became Presbyterian chaplain at Queen's University, that he sought ways to put those lessons into practice in his native land.

He had been present when an Irish student asked Karl Barth, the greatest theologian since Calvin, what people like him could do for world peace. Barth's answer was terse: 'Go home and set your own house in order.' That is what the dedicated band of Ulster people who founded Corrymeela did. Their testing time came early in the troubles, when Catholic families in West Belfast were caught in the crossfire between bands of terrorists and the security forces.

Ray Davey and his colleagues, mostly Protestants, whisked Catholic mothers and their families away from the troubled areas, where many feared their sons would themselves become involved with the IRA, and gave them a respite in their beautiful retreat on the North-eastern corner of the County Antrim coast.

This was a physical respite that was made memorable by the Christian love which accompanied it. It was a Catholic priest, a Holy Ghost Father from Dublin, who caught best the spirit of Corrymeela, after a visit there in 1972: 'On leaving the house, I met six young children coming up the road. Their father had been killed in the troubles a short time before. Their mother needed urgent hospital treatment, and it was Corrymeela that received these little victims of our politico-sectarian strife.

'Catholic orphans being cared for by young Protestant girls: a witness that our divisions are senseless, and that if we are divided, Christ is not.'

Corrymeela cannot provide a political solution to the problems of a community with two divergent national identities. It cannot provide a solution to terrorism. Those tasks must be done by politicians, soldiers and policemen. But if Europe is ever again to look to Ireland as 'the island of saints and scholars', the place from whose missionaries many parts of Europe learned their Christianity, it will be the spirit of Corrymeela which inspires the transformation of the human heart that is needed.

Once, when I was presiding at a conference at Corrymeela, attended by hard-bitten journalists and equally hard-bitten academics, I had – rather selfishly – had the seats arranged so that I would have a good view over the astonishing stretch of Atlantic water between Ballycastle and Rathlin. Ray Davey preached about these waters at the conference service. He spoke of the Vikings and Spaniards, pirates and missionaries, who had sailed through this turbulent strait down the centuries.

If there are to be fewer men of violence, and more people with the spirit of Christ in their hearts in Ireland, it is to people like those who created Corrymeela that we must look for continued inspiration.

John Cole
April, 1993

# *Point of Departure*

Ireland has two faces. I am reminded very poignantly of this when I stand on a promontory near Ballycastle on one of those special days when the sun is shining and all the beauty and colour of the sea and sky are limpidly clear. My vantage point is on the edge of a sloping lawn from which I can look far down to the crested waves breaking on the golden sand. Behind me stand the white walls and gables of the Corrymeela Centre which has worked for peace and reconciliation in Ireland since 1965. But my attention is drawn outwards across the turbulent waters of the Sea of Moyle to the L-shaped island of Rathlin, lying low in the sea and some seven miles away.

Beyond I can just see the dim outline of the Paps of Jura and further east the Mull of Kintyre and far away the mountains of Arran. Close at hand the massive headland of Fair Head with its long basaltic columns, rising at right angles from the sea, dominates the horizon. To me it is like the prow of some majestic ship pushing through the waves.

But even the luminous beauty of the landscape fills me with a wistful sadness as I remember all the cruel and tragic events that have taken place on these shores over the centuries. I think of all the different ships that have passed this way. The Vikings came in their longboats in the 5th century to plunder, capture and kill. In the 16th century the Spanish galleons passed by on their way to destruction. In the 18th and 19th centuries many ships sailed from these shores to the United States, driven out by political and religious persecution and later by the disaster of the Potato Famine. All these ships told of violence, fear, exile, persecution and destruction. Alas, the story continues, and still almost every township, village and city know the horrors of sectarian violence and killing.

But here in this same place above the sea I begin to think of that other face of Ireland. Those faithful men and women who over the centuries have moved through the villages and towns and lived and spoken the way of Christ's peace. Saint Patrick must have known these parts well in his journeys through Ireland, pointing out to those he met that there is a better way than hate and violence, and proclaiming the one true Peacemaker.

Forward again and Columba of Derry passed across these same waters in 563 AD. He and his twelve followers travelled in their coracle across to Argyll in Scotland and up the coast to Iona. Here they set up a great centre for learning and living the way of Christ, and disciples from here travelled all over Britain and far across Europe to tell their story of healing and reconciliation.

Corrymeela and the many other Christian communities in Ireland see themselves as spiritual descendants of Patrick and Columba. We seek to carry on their message. While so many things have vastly changed, the message of Christ the Prince of Peace does not change.

The citizens of Ballycastle are very proud of the fact that Marconi, the man who gave the whole system of radio transmission to the world, carried out one of his crucial experiments in Ballycastle in July 1898. Here he was able to transmit and receive radio signals from the ships that were passing by. This successful experiment completely transformed the whole world of radio communication. It rapidly developed and set in motion the vast network of radio and television which has revolutionized the lives of millions of people.

Communication! In a word this is what Corrymeela is all about. The perennial problem in Ireland is that still we are imprisoned in two camps. There has been very limited contact between the two. So we are captives of fear, ignorance and prejudice. We feel afraid and threatened by those in the other camp because we have never really talked to them.

The late Tyrone Guthrie, famed as a drama producer and critic and himself an Ulsterman, spoke to the point when he said: 'We were born apart, we lived apart, we worked apart, we never learned to come together . . . there was no institution to make it possible.'

At Corrymeela, when we say 'the Grace' together, joining hands, we ask for the communion of the Holy Spirit. Communion means communication and community. The Spirit is the unceasing communicator, seeking all the time to bring us into relationship with God and with each other. He is the animator, the go-between, the creator of insight and awareness. He is ever seeking to break down all the barriers that separate us, and bring us together as brothers and sisters in his one family.

So in our Corrymeela liturgy we declare:

'We are a community of the Holy Spirit.'

And we pray together:

'Spirit of the living God, fall afresh on me.
Spirit of the living God, fall afresh on me.
Break me, melt me, mould me, fill me.
Spirit of the living God, fall afresh on me.'

This is the unfinished story of a group of ordinary people in Ireland drawn from different Christian traditions, who over the last twenty-seven years have tried to respond to Christ's call to be channels of his peace in this broken and divided country. The journey has had many set-backs but in spite of uncertainty and disappointment it still goes on.

Long ago Columbus set out on his voyage in search of a new world to be discovered beyond the seas. It turned out to be a far more perilous and arduous journey than he had thought possible. There was much uncertainty about the route and at times mutiny was in the air. For weeks and months he made this simple entry in his log book: 'No land in sight, but sailed on.' That says it all for us. As yet we see no easy solutions or ready made answers, but we sail on in faith and hope.

# CHAPTER ONE

# *Formation*

*Time present and time past*
*Are both perhaps present in time future,*
*And time future contained in time past.* T.S. ELIOT

*(The Scotch-Irish) combined for much of their history a notable*
*liberalism with a strict severity of private discipline. They were a*
*serious people, caring for education, intent on self-improvement*
*and material progress, yet deeply marked by their religion. They*
*were kindly, humorous and at the same time austere, but always*
*responsive to their history which was at bottom a history of*
*frontier insecurity. Their mentality was essentially a seige*
*mentality.* F.S. LYONS, 'THE BURDEN OF HISTORY' LECTURE 1978

The huge banner, with its dramatic colours of orange, gold, black, red, purple and white dwarfed everything else in sight including, we felt, ourselves.

We were a group of children, a dozen in number, whose ages ranged from six to twelve years and the dusty hall with its heavy unwieldy furniture, across which the banner blazed, a gash of brilliant colour in our drab surroundings, was our school. There, in the local Orange Hall, Miss Maud Gamble, the sole teacher, ran a small private school. She had a continuous struggle daily to hold our attention, which was very limited in duration as we were so easily distracted. Our wide age range meant that we were at different stages of development and it was well-nigh impossible for her to hold our combined attention for more than a few minutes. Miraculously, Miss Gamble remained patient enough to take up the daunting task, day after thankless day, throughout my childhood years.

And then there was the banner of course, the king brandishing a sword, his horse poised ready for a fast furious charge. I used to wonder, as a six-year-old boy, whether the king's arm got tired holding the sword aloft all day and whether the horse would like to put his foot on the ground for a rest. But we needed no tuition in what the banner represented. The king was William III and he was at the river Boyne leading his men to attack the troops of King James II in the year 1690.

Close beside where we sat were the various impediments of the Orange Lodge: the ornamental standards, the flags, sashes, and the huge Lambeg drums. What an urge I had every time I looked across at them, to give just one wee quick 'dunder' when Miss Gamble's attention was elsewhere engaged.

Each morning she conducted school prayers. First we would sing 'Jesus, Friend of little children' or 'Jesus loves me'. Next, one of the older children read a short passage from the Bible and finally Miss Gamble led us in prayer. I cannot remember what she prayed about, but one phrase still stays in my memory, as it was used almost every day: 'O God, stay the hand of the assassin'. Of course I did not understand the big word, but I got the message all the same. For even then in the early twenties certain areas and roads close to Dunmurry were spoken of with bated breath, and the mysterious name 'shinners' (for Sein Fein) was mentioned only in a whisper.

'The village', as we always called it, was a neat and tight little community, with a deep sense of its own identity and distinctiveness from Belfast and Lisburn, between which it lay. As the youngest son I was very often sent to collect some needed items from the village shops. I was never instructed to go to the supermarket (they were still far ahead in the future) but to 'Jimmy Gray's' for a pound of butter. It was rather like one of the card games that was allowed, called Happy Families. What a marvellous group of characters we had in the village: Johnny Porter the plumber, Murtie Magee the butcher, 'Tib' Kerr the ubiquitous taximan with his 'Tin Lizzie' Ford, Wiltie Agnew the blacksmith with his Midas touch at his forge spouting great fiery sparks all around, Andy Bruce the barber in his saloon with spittoons specially located for the locals who dropped in for a shave and chewed tobacco as they waited their turn, and finally there was 'Patch-in-the-eye' the man who tarred the roads.

I was brought up in the manse, as my father was the Presbyterian minister in the village. Being close to Belfast the parishioners were from a wide variety of occupations. There were farmers, tradesmen, shopkeepers, office and mill workers, business and professional people and labourers working on the farms, roads and railway. My father had had a struggle in his youth as he was brought up in a small farm outside Carrickfergus and had worked his way through university to become a minister. This meant that he had a very real understanding of the people in his congregation and what many of them had to face in their jobs.

Both of my parents were not only involved in church work, but also in the life and needs of the wider community. It was not a 'privatized' religion but one that took in the whole of life as they experienced and understood it. I recently learned that my mother was responsible for starting the Guide movement in the village. My father also started a club for men (mostly unemployed) and later the Dunmurry Hockey Club. He was interested in all that went on in the community. Often he would try and get work for some unemployed person, or get involved in a campaign to persuade the railway authorities to build a bridge over the railway in place of the very dangerous open crossing.

He was a very keen supporter of the local football club and always took me along to the matches at Ashley Park very close to the manse. The team was a good one and drew large crowds on a Saturday afternoon to home games. Dressed in his black coat, dog collar and clerical 'soup plate' hat, he watched the game very intently and often unconsciously swung his right leg seemingly to urge the local team to greater effort.

At times the language of the spectators would be rather vivid and colourful, especially when the referee's decisions went against the home side. When anyone went too far he would receive a reproachful look from 'his Reverence', and very occasionally a verbal rebuke. The result tended to be that a *cordon sanitaire* formed within a radius of twenty to thirty feet from us, in which the language was suitably monitored. Even so they were well pleased to see him there, one of the crowd and one with them in their love of the game.

One Sunday morning I discovered that my one pair of boots was away at the mender's. I knew that I was expected to go to church. What could I wear? My mother suggested my slippers. I rebelled at this idea and complained that it would be 'sissy' going to church in slippers. Then I agreed that I would go, but on condition that I wore my football boots. This I did, and I am sure the Good Lord understood and perhaps even approved.

Involvement with the wider life of the village was taken for granted by our parents and I am sure it played a large part in my formation. There was little class consciousness and the village and surrounding countryside provided an exciting environment in which to grow up. My parents gave me a lot of freedom and a long rein. My elder brothers and sister would say that it grew longer as the family extended.

Two threads will appear right through this story: the importance of relationships and of community. The family is where both of these are created and developed. It is the embryo of all community. So I believe my family was a special gift to me. I do not suggest that we were angelic or saints-in-the-making. Far from it, as we had frequent tensions, clashes of interest and rivalry. But with all this diversity of temperament and outlook there was a deep unity of trust and support.

Each of the five of us made his or her own special contribution to the family. I think of my elder brother John as always a great encourager and supporter, so important to a much younger brother. Beth is the alive and aware one, always alert to new ideas and people. Will, the doctor, is the enthusiast and the committed one. Emily, the nurse, the caring one, also teaches us all to laugh.

My relationship to Emily is immortalized in a piece of engraving she, as a seven-year-old, did with a pinpoint on the mahogany mantelpiece in Dunmurry Manse. It is still to be seen.

She wrote this terse description of me: 'RAY IS A B . . .'. Fortunately there was parental intervention before the epigram was completed!

In those days nobody had ever heard of 'community centres' and yet we knew all about them. There was a two-acre field near the manse at the minister's disposal. My father, having retained his early interest in farming, kept a brown and white Jersey cow in the field. When the cow departed, the field changed roles and became a sports ground for the many boys who would arrive there after school. In summer our attention was transferred to the lawn in front of the manse, which became a multi-purpose pitch for cricket, hockey, football and tennis. I am amazed to remember how tolerant our parents were of these boisterous activities.

Yet it would be wrong to leave a picture of a rural paradise or a village utopia. There were many blind spots, and much was taken for granted. There was little awareness of 'the other side': the Catholic population. True, there were very few around the village and those who were there scarcely impacted our lives. We were aware of this deep division in our society, but in Dunmurry it seldom surfaced and any sort of ecumenism lay far ahead in the future. For the most part our elders talked little about it.

One regret I have now is that I did not make better use of the privileges I had in education both at school and university. I did pass the necessary examinations, but I can recall little intellectual excitement or stimulus in doing so. It was partly my fault and also the way we were taught, which was often dull and unimaginative. I have spent a good part of my later life in trying to 'restore the years the locust has eaten' in non-academic pursuits; not that I regret the times I spent at various forms of sport.

Not only did I find them an important part of my self-development, but also a marvellous opportunity to make friendships and relationships that crossed the barriers of background, religion and nationality. I was a very keen rugby player and had many opportunities of playing south of the border and across in England and Scotland. In this way I had many chances of widening my provincial outlook. At this period I realized that I was living in a very safe, protected environment, almost unconscious of the rest of society.

This had come home to me in my last term at school, at the Royal Academical Institution. I was sitting on my own in the prefects' room on the third floor. From my vantage point I had a very clear view of Great Victoria Street and the wide turn into Wellington Place leading from the city centre. Suddenly the early afternoon quiet was shattered by the angry shouts of men. They came and came, in a seemingly endless procession. They were poorly clad with 'duncher' caps and threadbare jackets. Many of them were carrying improvised banners and notices: 'We want justice not charity'. There was real poverty in the city with forty to sixty per cent unemployed as the building trade, shipbuilding and engineering industries were all idle. Benefits were very limited in order to encourage the unemployed to seek work. It was so bad that in this procession, and in many others, Catholic and Protestant, in their common vulnerability, combined to protest as the situation became desperate.

I was really shaken by that experience. I lived in Belfast with these same men, but had been completely insulated from their poverty, and my mentors and teachers had done little to make me conscious of it. Still today the chronic unemployment is one very important reason for the continuing violence. Soon after I took part in a camp for unemployed men in the Clandeboye estate near Bangor. This opened my eyes to the rejection and emasculation that a large number of my peers were experiencing.

It was not difficult to be a son of the manse. I am always grateful to my parents for the way they acted. They did not try to indoctrinate me, but rather created the atmosphere in which my inner faith could grow naturally. This was by the way they lived their own lives, how they were so wholeheartedly committed not only to the spiritual needs of the parishioners but also to their material welfare.

It was largely through my mother that my spiritual awareness developed. The trite phrase 'Christianity is caught not taught' was true for me. Her deep faith was expressed in her life. I am amazed how much time she gave to each of us in reading aloud the books of Dickens and Scott. Then there were the great spiritual classics such as *The Pilgrim's Progress* and many biographies of the great champions of the faith through the ages: the epic exploits of the Old Testament heroes, the journeys of St Paul, and the exploits of saints of the Church: Francis of Assisi, Bernard of Clairvaux and on to David Livingstone and Father Damien of the lepers. Nearer at hand she told of St Patrick and St Columba. We did not need any Goldwyn-Meyer extravaganza to release for us the drama and power of these heroic people of faith. She always wanted us to experience the positive and inspiring things of life. She knew that a supreme method of doing this was through the biographies of real people.

One small incident left a profound influence on me. The drawing room was the most attractive room in our manse. Early one summer morning the sun shone bright and clear through the large bay window looking out on a small lawn set off by trees and bushes in the background. A simple writing bureau sat in front of the window. As I passed silently along the hall the door was slightly ajar, and as I looked in I could see my mother sitting there very quietly. The sun gently illuminated the clear profile of her face. Her head was slightly tilted and I saw a look of deep calmness, serenity and peace. I knew then, even as a small boy, that it was real, and that the person she sometimes told me about was truly alive and present.

In 1937, having graduated at Queen's University in Belfast, I entered the Presbyterian Theological College nearby. Following the year there I opted to spend my second year in Edinburgh at New College. Finally I completed my theological studies back in Belfast for the last year. I was happy to break the three-year course with the middle one outside Ireland. I realized that I needed to experience a different environment and be away from home.

Edinburgh had many attractions and drew students from all over the world. I enjoyed learning about the great theological thinkers of the time. Barth and Brunner were very much on the centre of the stage. I was delighted to attend a course of lectures by John Baillie, the most eminent Scottish theologian of that time. In the future I was often to go back to the books, not only of John but also his brother Donald who at that time held the chair of Systematic Theology in St Andrews Divinity School. John was quite a formidable man, as I discovered some years later, when as chaplain at Queens University, I invited him to come to Belfast and be the special preacher at the University Centenary service. On the Saturday I took him for a drive to the Mountains of Mourne. In the course of our conversation I mentioned that I had just read his recent book *Invitation to Pilgrimage* and how much I had enjoyed it. 'Yes,' he replied, 'that was one of my simpler books.' I hastened to assure him that I had read some of the others.

Living in digs under the scrutiny of a Scottish landlady was one of my earliest experiences of the clash of cultures. Three of my Irish friends lived in digs in Comely Bank, and their very hospitable landlady always invited any of us visitors to stay for supper. One evening as a special treat she produced an immense haggis. We all tried valiantly to eat a small portion, but discovered we could not face it. One of our party, to his everlasting credit, saw this as a gross breach of manners and something that would hurt the good lady's feelings, and proceeded to consume the whole haggis himself.

In the summer at the end of the academic year I joined some other theological students in taking part in the Scottish Seaside Mission. Our team was to work in Ayr under the guidance of the Rev. D. P. Thomson, who was the inspiration of the whole project which included many other seaside resorts in Scotland.

One of DP's bright ideas was known as 'the Witness Box'. This was a small trestle rostrum with a platform about three feet high. My first week in Ayr coincided with the Glasgow Fair holidays, and the green by the beach was crowded with hundreds of visitors. No sooner had we erected the stand than the crowds surged around with curiosity. Then, to my utter horror, DP's eye fell on me and he said, 'You will be first to take the stand.' I was petrified, as up to that time I had spoken very little in public, and only to small groups and never in the open air. I mounted the stand, feeling like Raleigh as he climbed to the scaffold. I wondered if I would be able to open my mouth and utter anything.

DP was a large man with a much larger voice. He stood in the crowd eyeing me from five yards. There was a sudden lull and his mighty voice boomed across the Ayr Green: 'And who are you?'

My knees were beginning to knock, and I on the verge of profound embarrassment when suddenly, at the very last moment, words came to my lips. I looked calmly across in his direction, leant forward and, cupping my ear with my right hand, roared back at him: 'Can you speak a bit louder? I can't here you!'

That settled me, as the crowd exploded into laughter and cheers. It was plain sailing from then on. Whenever I think of direct inspiration, I always remember the Ayr Green in July 1938.

The most significant event of my year in Edinburgh was not to do with public speaking or theology, but rather with a visit I made one Wednesday afternoon to the University playing fields at Craiglockhart. It was not to play rugby, but to watch someone play hockey. She was Kathleen Burrows who had come over from Belfast to play for Queen's University Ladies' Eleven against the Edinburgh team. I am told that she was playing left-back. Truth to tell I remember very little about the match. But I do remember that I stood on the sidelines, contemplating a relationship that might develop. We were a sedate generation and did not move quickly in these matters, but the foundation was well and truly laid.

1938 and '39 were increasingly dramatic and threatening years for us all. I completed my studies, but everyone's attention was drawn more and more to the menacing events taking place in

Europe. Adolf Hitler was going from strength to strength, defying one government after the other. First he had occupied the demilitarized Rhineland, then Austria was annexed and, finally, Czechoslovakia. During August and September 1938 I was trying to study for a college scholarship. I found I could not concentrate. Study and examinations seemed so pointless at such a time.

The climax came when the Prime Minister, Neville Chamberlain, made his famous flight to Munich to meet Hitler. Then his triumphant return, waving 'the piece of paper' and claiming it was 'peace for our time'. It turned out to be a bit less than that – just one year in fact!

It was Sunday morning at 11:30 a.m. I was about to conduct my first service in First Bangor Presbyterian Church. I had only arrived there the day before, to take up duties as assistant minister. The church was packed out, some people standing at the doors. The atmosphere was very tense and strained. Just half an hour before the service everyone had listened to the Prime Minister speaking from Downing Street, telling the nation that we were now at war with Germany.

In the packed church many people were visibly moved, as some of them remembered the unending casualty lists of the First World War, especially close relatives and friends who had not come back. The younger people were stunned and shocked as they began to grasp what had happened and what it would mean.

This was for me a momentous occasion. So many events had come together, not only for me personally, but for our country and nation. It was my first duty in my first appointment. For everyone present it was the end of an old world and the tragic entrance of a new and very different one.

# CHAPTER TWO

# *In the Desert*

*A young Apollo golden haired*
*Stands dreaming on the verge of strife,*
*Magnificently unprepared*
*For the long littleness of life.* FRANCES CORNFORD ON RUPERT BROOKE

*You shall cross the barren desert,*
*But you shall not die of thirst.*
*You shall wander far in safety,*
*Though you do not know the way.*
*You shall speak your words to foreign men*
*And they shall understand.*
*You shall see the face of God and live.*

> *Be not afraid!*
> *I go before you always;*
> *Come follow me,*
> *And I will give you rest.* BOB DUFFIELD S.J.
> NORTH AMERICAN LITURGY RESOURCES

For me 1939/40 was a watershed and marked off very clearly the end of my formal education. In contrast to the easy flowing thirties – in many ways an idyllic time for me – the next five years were a complete contrast. They were swift-moving, dramatic and often traumatic: so much happened, so many shattering events and so many periods of deep uncertainty and ominous foreboding. Yet at the same time they were amazingly rich in extending my horizon: a collage of people, places and events.

Now my real education began. These years were powerfully formative and were to provide me with points of reference and perspective that are still much with me and evident at Corrymeela. I still struggle with and try to work out many questions that were first raised for me in that turbulent and exhilarating period. In spite of the years at university and theological colleges, I still felt inadequate, inexperienced and bewildered. I began to realize what a sheltered life I had lived and how insulated I had been from most of the realities of the wider world. The next five years began to lift the veil!

It was also a very unsettled time. The mould was beginning to crumble; the secure, predictable society in which I had grown up was coming to an end. Many of my university friends joined up and moved out of Ireland for training in the various services. The easy carefree atmosphere was replaced by a grim stoicism and solid determination to carry on and see it through. We got used to the blackout, food rationing, and even gas masks. These latter did, at least, provide an excellent substitute for false faces at Hallowe'en! There was a new civic responsibility and I remember enlisting for Red Cross and St John Ambulance courses. Some even studied the different types of gases with which we might have to contend. Hitler's massive columns had bypassed the Maginot line and broken through to the Channel. There had been the incredible evacuation from Dunkirk, but in our hearts we were all asking how soon would the Invasion begin, and what army could stop the armed might of Germany.

Always in the background was the devastation the U-boats were causing to Allied shipping in the Battle of the Atlantic. The cost of lives and ships was brought home to me when the first visit I had to make, as assistant minister in First Bangor Church, was to console parents who had just been informed that their son was missing. He was a crew member of the *Athenia* which had been torpedoed in mid-Atlantic. Up to this point the war had been remote. We listened to the news bulletins on the radio and talked about it. But now, in this event, it registered as I saw, face to face, what it meant to the relatives and friends. I'm glad to say their son did survive.

Since war became likely, and even when it was finally declared, I was not at all clear as to what I should do. I hated the whole idea of war, and, like many of my peers in the late thirties, had been influenced by the various pacifist movements. But now, as news of the concentration camps and the horrors of Nazi totalitarianism filtered through, I felt that I could not stay out of it. I decided like some of my friends to volunteer for field work overseas with the YMCA. I just missed Normandy, as Hitler arrived there first, but was posted to Egypt for service with the Middle East Forces.

So I set out from home on 27 September 1940. My emotions were very mixed. I wondered when I would see my parents again, as they were both quite elderly. At the same time there was a sense of excitement with apprehension, as I now had made the choice after long uncertainty. While I was sustained by the sense that this was right, I wondered what lay ahead.

Excitement and adventure came almost immediately, when our ten-ship convoy sailed out of the security of the Clyde into the open waters of the North Channel. Early in the morning a lone Heinkel bomber dived out of the clouds and aimed three bombs at our ship. Two of them missed, the other grazed the port side and exploded on the waterline, damaging the plates of the hull and putting the engines out of action. At the same time the decks were strafed and several soldiers killed and a number injured. Fortunately we stayed afloat, and after some very anxious hours the engines were started and we were able to return to the Clyde. Finally, after six weeks, we embarked on a convoy from Liverpool.

We were forty-eight days at sea as, with the Mediterranean blockaded by the Italians, we had to circumnavigate most of Africa. Stopping briefly at Sierra Leone and Durban before finally sailing through the Red Sea into the Suez Canal, we finally arrived at Port Said.

Those seven weeks, crowded as we were in the confined space of a troopship, were a learning experience for me. It was my first contact with life in the services and the complexities of the various groups of officers, non-commissioned officers, and other ranks. I was never sure just where I fitted in. My travelling companions were all considerably older than I was and had been established in business or professional life. Three of them lived in the south of England, two in London and the other in Cornwall. One of the Londoners had been in comic opera in the West End and the other a business executive. The third was an ordained priest of the Church of England but had never had a parish.

As the days passed and having to live in close proximity to each other, I had my first experience of 'cultural diversity'. I was the only representative of Northern Ireland. I realized, as never before, my Irishness. It came out in many ways: my accent, how I used words and pronounced them, the things that I laughed at and a deepening sense of my provincial background.

None of the others had ever been to Ireland and knew little or nothing about it and its divisions. I became aware of my identity and how much I differed from them. But it was reassuring, as the days passed and we talked together and got to know each other, to see how our differences grew smaller, as we discovered how much we had in common. Incidentally, one of the two Londoners, Harold Barker, became best man at our wedding after the war.

I also recognized that most people work on stereotypes about each other. The Irish tended to think of the English as self-assured, superior and rather looking down on the Irish, while the English thought of the Irish as 'Paddies', unpredictable and rather amusing.

Contemporary history has brought this question of cultural differences very much to the fore and it is very important in interpreting the Irish question. In any future political solution the cultural factor must be taken into account.

The eminent Irish historian, the late F. S. L. Lyons writes: 'Political solutions are indeed urgently needed, but they will be unavailing . . . if they go on ignoring the essence of the Irish situation which is the collision of a variety of cultures.'

When we arrived at Port Said on New Year's Day 1941 we were heartened to hear that Wavell's army was pushing Mussolini's forces back west across the North African desert coastline. Two of us were told that our job was to keep in touch with the Allied troops in their rapid advance. We would set up roadhouses for rest and refreshment along the lengthening lines of communication for those passing back and forward to the front. This for us marked the beginning of eighteen months of almost constant movement and change.

At the start it was a continual safari, as we ploughed across the desert, bumped over the broken sections of the road and camped at night. It was a new and exciting experience for us, for as yet we had found few problems. The first sobering reality was to meet huge convoys of Lancia lorries, filled with hundreds of Italian prisoners in their bottle-green uniforms. But even they did not seem to be downcast. Indeed many of them were singing their hearts out with relief that they were out of the war and would have the safety of a prison camp for the duration. That first impression of the Italians was fully verified when I was able to talk to them. Few of them had any heart for what they called 'Mussolini's war'.

Sometimes I would question what we were doing. We seemed to spend so much time travelling long distances, having engine trouble or getting bogged down in the sand. Then there was the perennial problem of supplies, as the distances from our base in Alexandria grew longer and longer. Was it worthwhile? One visit in particular helped to give me an answer.

I visited an anti-aircraft gun-site, deep down in the desert off the beaten track and miles from any mark of civilization. About a dozen men lived there to man the gun day and night and keep vigilant watch for enemy aircraft. The gun was dug in and encircled by a wall of sandbags. Inside the circle these men lived in small 'bivvy' tents and beside a slit trench. As I sat and talked to them I was able to share their feelings. The daily diet was bully beef and army biscuits, as supplies of fresh food were impossible in such an area. I could understand one of the reasons why I got a welcome, as I was able to bring them tinned fruit, chocolate and biscuits, as well as some books and magazines and a fresh supply of cigarettes.

I came to realize what it was like to live with the burning heat of the desert sun for a long part of the day. Continual perspiration and very basic shorts and shirt meant that large areas of the body were vulnerable to the attention of the myriads of flies, especially when there was food around. Other more personal things were even more difficult to accept: the infrequency of mail from home and family, anxiety about loved ones in the many blitzes in England and the long-term concern about the future and what lay ahead. For some, there was the agony of uncertainty about marital fidelity at home.

In addition there was the perpetual strain of living so closely together in a group from very different backgrounds and being tied day in and day out to the one small piece of desert. Above all, for them as soldiers there was the frustration of no action. One of them said to me: 'You know we've been here for more than two months and we have not even seen an enemy aircraft'.

Then I realized that our work was worthwhile. I understood what it meant to these men to see a different face, to talk to someone from outside and share anxieties about the folk at home and the uncertain future. I had often wondered if this was what I should be doing, as a trained minister. Now I realized how wrong I had been and that this was the right place to be. To be a minister is to be a servant, and where could I serve better than being with these men in their monotony, frustration and anxiety?

Towards the end of 1941 my pattern of life changed. Now, instead of travelling over vast areas of the desert, I was able to settle in one place. This was because the front line between the two armies had stabilized along the Gazala Line, about thirty miles east of the large naval base of Tobruk which the Italians had built as their main Mediterranean base before the war. It had successfully endured a siege in the first German push and after its relief by the Allied Forces earlier in the year became once again a vital base for thousands of troops within its ten-mile perimeter and along the Gazala Line, including the El Adem airport. This situation was a great challenge to the YMCA, as there were some thirty thousand men within the perimeter and many thousands along the Gazala Line which was within easy reach of Tobruk.

This meant that we could concentrate our energies in the town area and increase the service that had already been started during the earlier siege by Harold Barker and Hector Tankersley. The town itself had a grim forbidding atmosphere. It was built on a craggy promontory with its eastern side sloping down into a deep channel reaching out two miles to the open sea. This provided an ideal harbour and base for Mussolini's ambitions in the eastern Mediterranean. Indeed no other reason could have brought anyone here. There was nothing to soften the harsh environment. A few lonely palm trees in the town square did little or nothing to improve it. The harbour bay added to this gloomy atmosphere, as it had become a naval graveyard. Some thirty ships and submarines had been sunk there. Some were still partly afloat, including the Italian cruiser, *San Giorgio,* with her guns and deck still above water. Nearby lay the massive hulk of a 15,000-ton liner which had had to be beached there as the result of an unsuccessful attempt to run the gauntlet of the vigilant British artillery in an earlier battle.

Even so, with so many troops around the town and the wide perimeter, it was an ideal setting for the development of our work. I could see the possibilities of such a centre. There was no other place where the men could drop in for a rest and a change of company. As it developed, the Centre was able to respond not only to the physical and social but also to the spiritual needs of so many men, living under the demanding and ever dangerous conditions of desert warfare.

Here again I had to learn how to live under pressure. This was something I had not known in the spacious leisurely student years. Now I had many roles to play. At times I had to do accounts or plan the programme of lectures and concerts for the week. Then I had to drive out to visit units scattered across the forward areas. There were all sorts of unexpected visitors from generals to journalists, as well as troops from countries all over the world such as New Zealand, South Africa, France and India. It took me months to become attuned to the various accents of our own British tommies, the Geordies, the Cockneys, the Taffies, the Paddies, and the Jocks.

I had to learn patience, humour and tolerance, in addition to the ability never to get annoyed or shocked, even when I was utterly exhausted. I had indeed to be a man for all seasons. There were the other times when I had to lead the worship and share in a prayer or discussion group, listen to someone who wanted to talk, who was feeling the pressure and felt very isolated and vulnerable.

Another very important experience for me was the opportunity to meet so many chaplains and leaders from different denominations.

At home I had lived in a pan-Presbyterian world. Church relations were tentative and the ecumenical movement was still in its early stages. It is rather sad that it took such extreme circumstances to bring us together. For in the daily perils of desert war, denominational differences seemed to be insignificant. Here we were given the opportunity to support and encourage one another and share our resources and work together. In this way we came to know and appreciate each other's tradition and learn from our differences. In this situation I was able to meet representatives from all the levels of Anglicanism, Methodists, Congregationalists, Baptists, Roman Catholics, the Church Army, the Salvation Army, the Brethren and the Jewish community. Those meetings and that open atmosphere made a profound impression on me and left me very impatient with the tardiness of so much inter-church activity.

It was here I had the privilege of working with Harold Barker. He was one of the men I had met on the journey out from England. We had come to the desert together but it was here that I came to know his calibre. I can see now that he had a profound influence on my life. He was, to quote Sheila Cassidy's phrase, 'one of my icon people'. Time and time again I go back to the ideas I picked up from him. I had seen them worked out in what were to be the most demanding and difficult years of my life. It is at such times that superficialities are swept aside and real character emerges. We worked together for three unforgettable years.

Harold was ten years my senior and had been in the textile business in London and very much involved in youth club work in the East End. He was one of the most unselfish people I have ever met and never seemed to think about himself. At Tobruk we had constant air raids, as the Italian and German bombers tried night after night to knock out the harbour. He seemed to be unconcerned about these attacks and usually refused to join the rest of us on the ground floor, when the bombs started to fall. He had a great gift of relating to all the different officers and men who called in at the Centre. His morale seemed to rise as the bombs fell, and almost invariably he could see the funny side. Earlier he had been decorated for his work during the Siege of Tobruk and the citation read: 'Despite bombing and the unusual hardship of the Siege, he remained at his post, showing self-control and calm courage. He was at all times untiringly cheerful and ready to serve in any possible way.'

He was a man of profound faith and yet he was always prepared to listen to others whose beliefs were different from his. I learnt much from him about leadership. His type of leading was to motivate others by encouraging them to participate and try things out for themselves. He had a lovely tenor voice and a real feeling for music, yet the only time I heard him sing was in the choir at a service. Not for him the title role or the limelight. His task, as he saw it, was to persuade others to take the lead. Such was his theory of leadership and I have never forgotten it.

Early on we had created a small chapel room on the top floor. Prayers were held each morning and evening and a service each Sunday night. It had an atmosphere all of its own. I don't think I've heard better singing anywhere. The room was basically simple. The only Christian symbol was a painting of Mary and the Christ child which we had found in a bombed-out house nearby. The plaster walls were pitted with shrapnel and the window frames partly dislodged from their positions because of the continuous vibration and explosions from anti-aircraft batteries all around.

The chapel was in constant use by individuals who were glad to have a place where they could get away and have time to be on their own with the great luxury of quietness and stillness: time to rediscover the peace and presence of their God.

It was used by many different denominations. The Bishop of Pretoria held a confirmation service here. Roman Catholic priests used it for hearing confession, the Brethren met here, as did the Jewish rabbi. Members of the Friends' Ambulance Corps came here for quiet. I believed that such meetings of all these different traditions was right then, and hopefully it will become more the pattern for today.

That experience in the YMCA Centre in Tobruk has remained with me as a prototype of a meaningful Christian Community. It was located right at the place where life was lived in all its wartime pain, frustration and uncertainty. It was at the point where the need was greatest, where so many young men from so many different countries were, in their suffering and sacrifice, paying the price that is demanded when the nations can find no other way of settling their conflicts. It seemed to me a blood sacrifice they were asked to pay for all the greed and pride of the most wealthy and cultured nations in the world.

The Centre became a place where many came to unburden themselves, to talk about their hopes and fears, their sorrows and anxieties, the responsibilities they had to carry and the decisions they had to make. This Desert Community did fit into John Mackay of Princeton's description of the Christian community as 'a place where life is lived most closely to man's need'.

I will never forget one young officer who dropped in to the Centre one day. He just wanted to talk to someone. I was immediately impressed by him. He seemed to have everything: looks, physique, intelligence and charm. He told me he was a tank officer and had just come out of a very fierce battle in a place most appropriately called 'the Devil's Cauldron', some twenty miles from the town. Here the tanks drew up and literally stood and tried to blow each other to pieces. Then he went on to tell me what it felt like and how much he hated it all. He spoke of his deep Christian faith. He went on to describe the overwhelming desire he had: 'Do you know what I would love to do?' he said. 'I would love to get out of my tank and go across and shake the hand of the German commander.' Soon after, he left and I never saw him again. But that brought home to me in an unforgettable way the terrible tragedy and contradiction of it all and the price that a whole generation were asked to pay.

At this time I began to think of what I should do. Should I stay in the YMCA? I had now been in the desert eighteen months. It had been worthwhile, especially the last spell in Tobruk. I began to ask myself if I should move on to some other type of service. I talked to several Army and RAF chaplains and they told me there was a shortage of men and that I should apply. One of the things that attracted me was the chance of being attached to one unit, living with them, moving with them, getting to know them and building a relationship with them.

There was only one problem, should I decide to make this move. In my hasty departure from home I had missed my ordination. I knew it would not have been right to travel away back home for this at such a crucial time in the war. My friends at home, therefore, in my Belfast Presbytery, arranged with the Church of Scotland that I should be ordained in Jerusalem by their Middle East Presbytery. What an inspiring thought it was – to be ordained in Jerusalem of all places! But life, especially in wartime, is full of surprises and I was about to experience the biggest one of my life.

# CHAPTER THREE

# *Prison*

*By the rivers of Babylon, there we sat down, yea, we wept . . .*
*How shall we sing the Lord's song in a strange land?*
PSALM 137:1–4

*Return to your stronghold, O prisoners of hope.* ZECHARIAH 9:12

'*Raus*', '*Händer hoch*' were the threatening orders of the German soldier of the Afrika Korps who suddenly burst into our YMCA Centre. We had little choice, as he brandished his automatic weapon and began to use its butt to push us towards the exit. It was 6:30 p.m. on 20 June 1942. We had been prepared for evacuation by land or sea, but never capture. There had been a lot of shelling and gunfire near the town and then a long period of quiet. No messages had come from Area Headquarters – our usual source of information. True, stray soldiers had come to the Centre with alarming reports of the German advance. But somehow we had refused to think about this possibility. Now it was a stark fact as we began to leave the YMCA, holding our hands above our heads. There was no time to snatch even a few items of clothing and small kit. This was obviously not a time for requests or discussion.

As we marched down to the main piazza at the town hall, we were all still in a daze. Even a short street battle close at hand seemed to be unreal and imaginary. One young German crouched with his machine gun looked up and taunted us with the time-honoured phrase: 'For you the Var is over . . . Now it is a long vay to Tipperary.' Our line of prisoners was ever-extending, as more and more men filed out of the various buildings along the street. I saw a sailor with a tiny little black and white dog. It had already been in the wars, as it had only three legs. Its name was Stuka and it seemed to share our bewilderment, but trustingly fell into the file beside its master to face what lay ahead.

In a strange way our capture was a relief. The tension and suspense had passed and soon everyone began to chatter and even laugh, as we adjusted to this new situation. Now we had plenty of time to understand what had happened so unexpectedly to change our lives. Our fate, with that of 30,000 others, had been sealed by Field Marshall Rommel and his tanks unexpectedly being able to breach the perimeter defences and take the Allied forces by surprise.

We had to sit in the square for several hours as more and more prisoners arrived, including many that I knew. There was a sense of wry amusement, and all sorts of experiences were described, as well as speculation about the future. We were sharply brought back to reality, as we had to sleep in the open with a cool breeze blowing in from the sea and no blankets to keep in the heat. In addition we began to feel hungry. Early in the morning we were moved to the grounds of the Tobruk hospital.

Food was very short and with all the dislocation there seemed little chance of any. Then a Good Samaritan in the person of an Army Padre called Naylor, produced some tea for our small group from the hospital. Later he returned with a blanket, a bar of Lifebuoy soap, some bread and a small New Testament. Surely the basics for the simple uncomplicated life that lay ahead!

After two endless days in a sand-swept desert cage we were divided into groups of forty and packed into huge open Lancia lorries. Our new life had begun. It was very fortunate that Harold Barker, Fred Hill – young 21-year-old Salvation Army Officer – and I were able to keep together, as we were able to support each other in the days ahead. Barker, as ever, was able to see the humorous side of it all.

Amazingly the readjustment only lasted for a few days. Life began to fall into a pattern set by meal times, sleep and endless speculation about the future. Of course we were told that we were in transit camps and all would be well when we settled down in Italy. All I can say is that the transit stage never seemed to end. A vast amount of time was spent in waiting for the next move. There were several things that kept me going, mainly the support of my friends. In addition there was a sense of curiosity in seeing 'the enemy' face to face. It was quite a shock to realize how much I had been influenced by the stereotypes of propaganda. I had expected our captors would be ruthless and hard. A few were like that, but for the most part they were so like any of us and shared our frustration and war weariness. Some even had a fatalistic attitude – 'You today, me tomorrow, who can tell?'

As I adjusted to the new life there were two very positive and sustaining thoughts in my mind. I realized that this was going to be a tremendous experience for me. I also saw it as a challenge, the biggest one I had had to date. It was not only a physical but also a mental and spiritual test. Now what I thought I believed was being put to the test. My whole character and beliefs were to be tried in this prison crucible. I realized how comfortable and secure my life had been at home and now in the restrictions, deprivations and pressures of prison life the challenge had come. Stephen Spender's lines catch something of what I was to go through:

> What I expected was
> Thunder, fighting
> Long struggles with men
> And climbing.
> After continual straining
> I should grow strong;
> The rocks would shake
> And I would rest long.
> What I did not foresee
> Was the gradual day
> Weakening the will,
> Leaking the brightness away.
> The lack of good to touch,

The fading of body and soul
Like smoke before the wind
Corrupt, unsubstantial.

There was another thought that was to last through the coming years and sustain me. Before capture I had always felt that there was a certain intangible barrier between myself and the soldiers I lived with: the sense that I was only on the edge of their daily lives. I was a civilian and not exposed in the same way to the pressure, frustrations and in some cases the danger that they had to face. But now I was completely one with them. We were all in it together. That to me made all the difference. Most of the time there was little that I could do or say. But it was important just to be there with them, to listen and understand and at times to share their weakness and vulnerability.

We moved through several prison camps in Italy. These were all for non-commissioned soldiers and were, to put it mildly, basic and primitive. There was much inefficiency on the part of those who detained us. Food was minimal and living in a huge factory shed with several hundred others in three-tier wooden bunks was a crash course in learning to co-exist. Red Cross food parcels, when they came, were life-savers. But human beings are adaptable and any sociologist would have had a marvellous case study of how society can develop in the most testing circumstances.

Again it was here the gift of a small Christian group that kept me going. I am sure that it was the main reason why I was able not only to survive but to learn and grow. This group put its energy into planning Sunday services as well as identifying ways in which we could be of help to any prisoner in special need. This was very important for us. Not only did it put us on our mettle, but encouraged us, when we were depressed, to look outward beyond ourselves. This was crucial for us all. There was the constant temptation to look inwards at one's own problems and pressures – the hunger, cold, and crowded conditions. But the unfailing remedy was to keep looking outwards beyond ourselves to the needs of others.

Each one of us found his own level of operation. We were able to help in the education programme. I was responsible for elementary Latin! Barker and Hill used their musical skills, one running a choir and the other playing his accordion. There was plenty to do, if you opened your eyes.

One of my ploys was to go into the camp hospital, where the morale was low. There were very few books, so I followed the BBC example and read 'A Book at Bedtime'. I started each evening at 7 p.m. and continued reading aloud for an hour. One book turned out to be very popular. It was Agatha Christie's detective novel 'Ten Little Nigger Boys' In unravelling the mystery of her plot, the identity of the murderer is left to the last page. I was rather pleased at the rapt attention the patients gave to the readings, especially towards the end. Disillusionment followed later, when I learnt that the reason for this very special interest was the side bets that each one had put on the identity of the criminal.

I have already spoken of my icon people. I met up with one of these in this Italian camp. He was a Methodist chaplain called Douglas Thompson. His earlier life had specially equipped him for this daunting task in a prison camp. He had been a missionary in China for twenty years and had practised psychotherapy, a training that came into its own in a camp of 2000 prisoners. He had an ability to meet men at their own level. He knew very well that only a fraction of the prisoners were churchgoers. But he also knew that most of them had only recently been married, or were engaged or hoped to be married after the war. So he gave a series of lectures on 'Christian Marriage'. In developing this almost universally popular course, he was able to present the importance and relevance of Christian values and faith in such men-women relationships.

Another special concern he had was for the group of some twenty Jews in the camp. There was no rabbi and they seemed to be very much on their own. So Padre Thompson decided that something had to be done. He ran a study of the Old Testament prophet Hosea. He chose this book because he believed it to be the high-water mark of the Old Testament. Gomer, Hosea's wife, sold herself into prostitution. It would have been judged right and proper for him to have thrown her out. Hosea thought of this and suddenly realized that God had not done this to His people Israel in spite of their infidelity, but had gone on loving and caring for them, though they spurned and rejected him. Padre Thompson felt that if they and we could really understand the story of the prodigal daughter of Samaria we could also understand the prodigal son of the parable. Those days under the mulberry trees in Camp 70 were very special for me and many others. Several went on for ordination when they arrived home.

It was here that I came to understand and experience the sacrament of Holy Communion in a deeper way. It was not just the words but the action. Here I recognized the truth of Goethe's words that 'the highest cannot be spoken: it can only be acted'. Just after Reveille on Sunday morning we came together in the corner of a huge bleak factory shed. We each brought a blanket to sit on, as there were no chairs. The only furniture was a roughly made table covered with a grey blanket. On this the elements of bread and wine were laid out beside a simple wooden cross. We each had saved a piece of bread from our meagre ration of *pane*. These were gathered on a plate which a prisoner had fashioned from empty Red Cross tins. So also the cup which held some Italian *vino*.

What a motley bunch we were! Long since our desert shorts and bush jackets had worn out and had been replaced by ill-fitting bottle-green Italian pantaloons. Mine only reached halfway down my calf. Likewise the tunic sleeves were several inches short. It was midwinter, there was no heating and it was cold. Life for all of us was at its lowest level and food was very short.

Yet as we gathered round that table and shared the bread and wine and thought of what they meant, each of us felt a profound sense of peace, healing and hope in our hearts. We listened, as the Padre said: 'Hear what comfortable words our Saviour Christ saith unto all that truly turn to him . . . Come unto me all that are heavy laden, and I will refresh you'. We knew that they were for us!

Still many twists and turns lay before us in our journey. There were those final days in Camp 70 when we seemed to pass through the whole spectrum of emotion. There was the ecstatic hope when in September 1943 the Allies landed in the south and began to advance. Then the Italians capitulated. In our excitement home and freedom seemed very near. Then the long slow agonizing hours and days of suspense and rumour. Finally the utter despair when, instead of the Allies, a flying column of German paratroopers arrived and surrounded our camp and dashed our hopes and dreams.

Soon with Teutonic efficiency we were packed into cattle wagons marked for '40 men or 8 horses'. We had 49 in our vehicle! Then followed six claustrophobic days of travel. I am told we passed along the east coast of Italy, on to the Brenner Pass and through the Alps. Next we crawled across Austria and into south Germany and arrived in Saxony. Then the limbo of two transit camps. On New Year's Day 1944, I suddenly emerged into a new life, when I was appointed chaplain to a large group of work camps, located in Dresden and neighbouring towns and villages, known as Stalag 4A. This was almost a reincarnation, because my job and my parish were now clearly marked out for me and opened a new challenge.

I lived in an ancient castle in Hohnstein, a little mountain village in the Harz mountains about ten miles from Dresden. My main task was to visit some eighty camps and two hospitals in the Stalag area. According to the Geneva Convention military personnel under the rank of sergeant were obliged to work. These 'duty trips', as the German authorities called them, turned out to be unforgettable for me. I would set out with my armed escort to do a tour of six to ten days, to visit one district with a group of camps fairly close together. I stayed in each camp overnight, so had time to talk with most of the men. These *Kommandos* were usually attached to a factory or public works which ranged from cement-making, coal mining, chemical processing, to railway and post office depots. Each camp 'employed' from twenty to two hundred prisoners.

Travelling round Dresden and beyond in slow overpacked trains with continuous air raids was an amazing experience. I found myself deeply saddened both by what I saw and heard. I felt like an intruder, indeed an alien intruder, watching the agonizing death-throes of Hitler's Reich. I can still see the pale emaciated faces of the factory workers, leaving Hohnstein on the 5 a.m. train for their work in Dresden, each with his navy-blue peaked cap and thin shiny jacket, shivering in the cold mountain air. Each clutched his 'hand case', in which he carried his frugal breakfast of black bread, flavoured with a piece of garlic spiced sausage. They were a picture of apathy and despair.

These journeys were becoming more and more hazardous as the Allied bombers penetrated into the east of the country. On one journey a small boy became very tired and restless during one unusually long delay. The harassed mother tried to pacify the child by saying: 'If you don't keep quiet the bombers will come.'

They all knew that the writing was on the wall for their country and, with this knowledge, there was a pathological fear of the Red Army who were now beginning to move in from the east.

Of course the reason for my journeys was to visit the various camps in the Stalag. In this I played several roles. I was able to act as liaison between the Stalag headquarters and the individual camps. I had to deal with requests for study books, sports equipment, musical instruments, which the various international agencies in Geneva supplied. Then there was personal counselling, for folk at home, unsteady marital relationships, lack of letters, serious illness or bereavement. Travelling round the various camps, I was able to pass on news and greetings from and to mates that had been separated. In addition, I usually had very recent information on the war front.

The official description of my activity was 'spiritual comfort' and a central purpose of my visit was to hold services. This I did in every camp and usually in addition I celebrated Communion. Most of the men would attend. I realized that few of them were churchpeople. I tried to speak as directly and honestly as I could. It was vital to speak about the realities of their everyday existence, the difficulty of faith in such circumstances, and how these years of captivity could be used in a positive way. I had to grapple with the problem of religious language and concepts. I could identify with their inner feelings, their hopes and fears, because they were mine also. Unfortunately my visits were few and it was difficult to build relationships. Again I could see the importance of those small groups of prisoners in some of the camps who took a Christian stand, organized regular services and were able by their example and witness to make the faith real for those around them. I did all I could to support such efforts. Usually the prisoners who took part in these Christian 'cells' had to accept a lot of banter, but underneath there was great respect and admiration for those who took this stand.

There were those times of great sadness when in the four months at the end of 1944 and the early part of 1945, I had to conduct the funerals of twenty-four prisoners. Most of them had been killed in accidents at work, in the frequent air raids and several by exhaustion and hardship when they had to evacuate their camps in the east of the country and try to march west in the frost and snow of winter. How hard on their relatives and friends that they had survived three, four or five years of war and this should happen so near the end! As I took part in those funerals I admired the dignity and fortitude of the prisoners. But I could not help thinking of what this tragic news would mean to distant homes in South Africa, America and the British Isles. Those mothers, wives and children whose minds were buoyed up with the hope of homecoming and reunion!

But for me, there were always those little annunciations that kept turning up in these shattering and demanding days: those very special people who came along at the right time to revitalize my faith and restore my spirit.

Frau Gertrud Weisheit was the dentist in Hohnstein. I first met her when I was allowed, as a protected person, to have short walks round the village. I learned from a Belgian prisoner that she would be glad to welcome me to her home. She was strongly anti-Nazi and encouraged me to listen to the BBC news. This was a capital offence at the time. I could then pass it on to the other prisoners. She helped me to understand the dilemma that the Hitler regime presented to many Germans who wanted no part in National Socialism.

Her husband, who shared her opinions, had to join the army, and she had had no word of him for almost two years. Her young son of eighteen had been forced to join the SS and go to the Russian Front from which he never returned. She was left to carry on at home and look after her sixteen-year-old daughter, Siegrid, and Christian, a little six-year-old boy. In spite of all the burdens she carried, she was a remarkably serene and unselfish person. She was a great source of strength to many other prisoners and people around her in the village.

I will never forget one visit I paid to her. As I listened to the BBC news, she provided a cup of coffee. I knew she was the organist in the village church and we began to talk about music and various hymns. Then Siegrid said to her: 'Why don't you sing a Bach Chorale for Pastor Davey?'

In her beautiful clear soprano voice she sang, 'Jesu, Joy of Man's Desiring'. As she sang, my thoughts went back to home when my sister Beth, and also the choir, had so often sung this same chorale in our Dunmurry church. The memory of that visit sustained me for a long time after.

Quickly now the war moved to its tortuous conclusion as the German resistance in the east crumbled before the Russians. Refugees in desperation took the road to the west and soon Dresden was filled with them. Added to the fear of the Russian advance there was the perennial question: would the British and Americans mass-bomb Dresden? The inhabitants rationalized among themselves and often they would say to me: 'The British and Americans are cultured people and surely would never attack this great city of art and culture with very few industries. After all, this is the city of Bach, Handel and Telemann. Some of Wagner's operas were first staged here. Goethe, Schiller, Ibsen and Dostoyevski all lived here. In addition there are those priceless gems of Baroque architecture and, of course, Dresden china. Who would want to destroy such things? After all is not Dresden the Florence of the Elbe?'

What a devastating shock lay ahead of them and one whose strategic necessity and morality are still hotly debated fifty years on!

CHAPTER FOUR

# *Freedom*

FATHER FORGIVE

These words are carved in stone over the altar and below the Charred
Cross in the ruins of Coventry Cathedral, destroyed by bombs on
15 November 1940.

*When Yahweh brought Zion's captives home*
*at first it seemed like a dream;*
*then our mouths filled with laughter*
*and our lips with song.* PSALM 126:1, 2 JERUSALEM BIBLE

It was strange going back to Dresden with Kathleen in May 1985.
I was asked to be one of the four members of a British Council
of Churches group to attend a gathering of Christians from the
different nations involved in the war. It was organized by the East
German Churches and was to meet in Berlin. Dresden was not
on our schedule, but I said that I would travel provided I was
able to go back and visit it again. The Germans graciously agreed
and planned a visit for us.

Why, I asked myself, was my desire to return so strong? Was
it to let Kathleen share in these past experiences, or was it
something more? Was there still some unfinished business on my
mind? A sense of guilt that I had not really taken in what had
happened, or had not felt, as fully as I should, the agony, pain
and horror of what the inhabitants had gone through? I had been
so suddenly removed from it all. One thing I did know, I really
wanted to return and see it all again and find out what had
happened to some of those I had known. The pastor of the
ancient Kreuzkirche in Dresden and his wife, Christof and Maria
Ziemer, could not have been more sympathetic and hospitable.

At the end of one meeting with about twenty German pastors,
one elderly man came up to greet me. He was most friendly and
sensitive and, as he greeted me, he handed me a small paperback

book, *The City before THE NIGHT*, written by a well-known German author, Karl Josef Friedrich. It very vividly described the everyday life of the city on the eve of February 13th 1945. It outlined the devastating events of that night and the following day with its indescribable aftermath.

Afterwards I began to ask myself just why he had given me this book. I was sure that it was not with any sense of malice or bitterness. I believe he wanted to remind me what it had meant to the lives of thousands of ordinary people and how the memory of that suffering and loss still lives on after such a long time.

But how could I ever forget those two days when I had been visiting the various prison camps in Dresden? Many prisoners were arriving from the east force-marched before the Red Army's advance into the Reich. Prisoners had been compelled to march in the depth of winter to Dresden. Many were utterly exhausted and frostbitten. I had wanted to stay in the city and do what I could. But my guard had insisted that my temporary permit finished on the morning of the 13th, and therefore I must return with him to Hohnstein on the train at 2 p.m.

I was just back in our Castle headquarters when the raid on Dresden began. I wrote in my log:

> The first alarm went about 10 p.m. Flares already illuminated the whole landscape and made it clear as daylight. The ominous roar grew louder and louder and closer and closer. Later we learnt there were 1500 planes on the raid. The noise was deafening and the sentries rushed round swearing and shouting. They pushed us down into the basement with fixed bayonets. We heard the continuous crunch of the bombs and we knew that Dresden's time had come. Peace and quiet gradually returned after an hour. This silence accentuated the vast eerie light far across the sky.

At length we settled down for sleep, but it was not to be as another wave of bombers arrived to repeat the performance an hour later. Next day at midday the American bombers arrived to complete what came to be called the Triple Blow. Even so, we were ten miles from the city and did not grasp the full reality of what had happened.

I was not allowed to visit Dresden for two weeks, in which time the full picture had been toned down. The thousands of bodies had been removed. Estimates of the dead range from 35,000–200,000. The true figures will never be known, as the city had been invaded by many thousands of refugees from the east.

One place, the Hauptbahnhof – the Central Station – summed up the horror of it all for me. Here was a place I had passed through so many times with different guards. It had been so busy and throbbing with life. Now there was an unearthly quiet. One or two people wandered about aimlessly. The inside structure seemed to have collapsed and looked like a massive scrap yard. The synchronized clocks bore mute witness that destruction had descended at 22 hours 57 minutes. The station was elevated, with two tiers of platforms and a large basement below at street level, where thousands of refugees from eastern Germany slept at night. It was estimated that 16,000 perished that night in the station. No one bothered with me or my guard, as they wandered round in a daze mutely waiting for the end.

The events of those days are etched on my mind for always. I am sure that was one reason I wished to go back with Kathleen after forty years.

There was one experience which was for me 'a healing of memory'. It was Rogation Sunday and Christof Ziemer asked if we would both take part in the service. Kathleen read one of the lessons and I was invited to explain why I had come back. I had nothing prepared and just spoke from the heart, telling the people how I felt. I explained that the last time I had been in their city I was a prisoner and an enemy. I told of the suffering and loss of many of my colleagues, and how some had died of exhaustion and exposure due to the forced marches. Then I went on to tell of the horror and outrage many of the prisoners had felt as they saw the terrible aftermath of the massive bombing. I ended what I had tried to express as follows: 'But now today, at this Table, we all meet together to share this bread and this wine. In doing so we experience the Presence, the Forgiveness and the Healing of our One Lord and Master. "For He is our peace and has broken down the dividing wall of hate and made us one people".'

I knew then why I had wanted so much to come back, to be there with those people of Dresden, at the one table, with the One Christ. I also believe that I was speaking for a vast number of my fellow prisoners-of-war.

Later on our hosts took us to the famous Dresden Opera House, the Semper Oper. It had been very severely damaged in the raids and had just been re-opened a few weeks before on the 40th anniversary of the 1945 attacks. The same opera, Karl von Weber's *Der Freischutz* was being played as on the fatal night.

During the interval, when the lights went up, a lady next to Kathleen began to talk to her. She explained how she and her husband had been at the service and recognized us. It had meant much to them both. They had come over from Munich, where they now lived, on a four-day visit. They decided to go to the Kreuzkirche because her husband had been confirmed there. At the time of the raids he was in the army, though he was only sixteen years old, and living away from home in barracks. During that night his mother, his six-year-old brother and both grandparents were killed. Ever since, he had been filled with hatred against the British and Americans, and vowed he would never forgive them. But that day at the service he felt, for the first time, that he could forgive.

Unfortunately at that point the theatre lights were dimmed as the opera continued. Then at the end in the rush we missed them and I felt very sad that I had not been able to talk to him. As we left the theatre, we were soon merged in a large crowd with many cars moving off. Suddenly a man appeared dodging through the traffic. He grasped me by the hand and, as I wrang his, I asked for his name. He replied that his name did not matter. He just wanted to shake my hand. He held it fast for a moment. I could see that there were tears in his eyes, and all he could say was, 'Now I can forgive', and then he rushed away, to be lost in the crowds.

It was easy to use the word 'forgiveness' at such a time. But what did it mean? Who forgives whom? It is so easy to get into a tit-for-tat situation. What about the bombing of London and Coventry? What, then, about Berlin and Hamburg? What about the Nazis and the concentration camps? But what about the Versailles Treaty and devastating reparations after World War I? There is only one place where we can go beyond the military and political arguments, and that is at the Table before the Cross of Christ. Here we meet on level ground. We recognize that we are all guilty, we are all in it together, both as nations and individuals. So the only prayer we can pray is 'Father forgive – each one and all of us.'

The few weeks of waiting after the bombing were a terrific strain. What was going to happen, as the Red Army moved in towards Dresden and the Allied bombers commanded the skies above us? Around us was the demoralized German army. We were in the middle. In fact the Allies and Russians first met at Torgau, very close at hand, on the Elbe.

Still we were kept in our castle and, surprisingly, from time to time I was allowed to visit camps where a prisoner had died or been killed. It was a very tense and anxious time, and some camps had run out of food.

I wrote this prayer in my log at the time:

18 April 1945.
Father, these are tremendous yet difficult days. The spirit of hope is in the air, yet it is mingled with suspense, anxiety and strain. We know not what each morning will bring forth. Rumours and alarms excite us by day and disturb us at night. We turn in

confidence to you. Through all the changes and chances of wartime and prison life you have been our Guard and Guide. Your unseen Presence has given us strength and patience, and when hope burned low you have walked before us. And now we make the old surrender of ourselves, our fears and our doubts. Lead us on now and bring us in your good time out of the darkness of this long captivity to the light of freedom and home, where we will serve you with a more understanding love. Amen.

At last on the third day of May, the Kommandant told us to prepare to move out the next morning. I will never forget the 4th, the almost uncontainable excitement and relief I felt. At last the great day had come, after almost three years in captivity, and a further two in the desert. The massive gates of the castle were wide open, all the barriers down and most of the Germans had vanished except for the few who wished to go with us and, if possible, get away from the Red Army.

It seemed, as we walked away downhill from that mountain village, as if nature itself was celebrating with us. The apple blossoms were in full bloom and the fresh green grass of early summer everywhere. Many of the villagers turned out to see us leave. We knew that most of them were victims just as we had been. I felt a real sadness, as I wondered just what lay in store for them. I thought especially of Gertrud Weisheit and her family, who had been so kind to me. What would happen to them now, as the Russian troops began to arrive?

The days that followed were like a speeded up movie, as so many changes took place. First of all, we set out on the road to find the Allies, but only succeeded in walking right into the Red Army. It was a dramatic encounter, as the Russians had just finished a battle with a fanatical German SS division in a town called Teplitz in the Harz mountains. We were so preoccupied that we hardly listened to a woman passing by, who shouted, *'Der Krieg ist aus'* — 'The war is over'. How relieved we were to see white sheets and flags hanging out of the windows, although some shells fell quite close.

We had run right into the Russian army, but fortunately they realized who we were, and allowed us to pass through. At last the great moment came, as our road began to fill up with all sorts of Allied prisoners. Some in cars, buses, tractors and bicycles, but all going in the one direction. Someone shouted, 'Here come the Yanks', and a long line of jeeps came into sight. There was no time for celebration and we were promptly told to go on to Karlsbad where we would get further instructions. There we found ourselves in the efficient hands of General Patton's army.

I reported to a very pleasant American major in a transit camp. I noticed that on the floor of his office, he had a huge stack of all sorts of revolvers that had been confiscated from German officers. He looked at the pile, then turning to me he said: 'Say, would you like a gat?'

I thanked him as politely as I could and, as I declined his offer, I said: 'I have come through the war this far without a gun and I do not need one now.' I hope I was not rude, but I just did not want one. I have always been rather scared of guns anyway!

The next day, May 13th, we all sat on a bank on the edge of the Nuremberg airfield. It was very early in the morning and our bus had lost its way and we had had little sleep. But we were standing by for repatriation to England via Brussels. Everyone was silent as we waited. I remember that it had been such a day as this almost three years ago, when I had waited at the Benghazi airfield to be flown to further captivity in Italy. It was fitting to go back home in the same way. The air filled with the music of great Dakotas from England slowly dropping from the sky on to the airstrip. As I saw them descend, the lines of an old Negro spiritual kept ringing in my mind:

Swing low sweet chariot, coming for to carry me home.

Soon we were aboard and the great plane rose into the cloudless sky. I was glad to sit back and relax in the comfort of the soft seats. What a luxury it was just to rest and listen to the steady hum of the engines and let my mind begin to wander back over the past five years, an opportunity that had not come my way for a long time. A great weariness came over me as I thought of all the sadness, suffering and tragic destruction I had seen; the endless lines of refugees, especially the old and the mothers with children, and no place to go. I thought of those who had been kind to me and helped me in difficult times. Then there were those who were not with us, whose bodies lay in desert or in Italian and German graves. Their loved ones would have no joyful celebrations.

My heart began to fill with gratitude for all I had received and learnt: the people I had got to know, the friends I had, the experiences I had passed through and how I had escaped injury and ill health. I thought of one of the hymns we had so often sung on the way on the Andes troopship in 1940:

> Guide me, O thou great Jehovah,
> Pilgrim through this barren land;
> I am weak, but thou art mighty:
> Hold me with thy powerful hand.

My thoughts moved on, and I had a dialogue with myself. 'Are you a better person? What have you learned from these crowded years?' Even now I find it almost impossible to answer such questions. I certainly learnt much about myself and I came to realize how much I had still to learn. The experiences of those years still live with me, and will not go away. They are like delayed-action fuses that constantly go off in my thinking and still hold before me challenges that I have to face. The insights that they gave me, and the tried and tested models, continue to inspire me today. Browning's lines express the feelings I had at the time on the homecoming plane:

The future I may face, now I have proved the past.

So my thoughts swung to the future and going back home: the untiring support and love of my parents, brothers and sisters given through the long five years. I remembered their constant letters and occasional parcels. Their thoughts and prayers had been a great anchor for my life. I imagined what my brothers and sisters had also gone through in wartime: John, a missionary in India with so many concerns and responsibilities in his life there; in Edinburgh my sister Beth, on the staff of St Colm's Missionary Training College; and my brother Will, a surgeon in the Air Force and one of the first doctors to land in Normandy on D-Day. Emily, my young sister, had been a nurse in the St George's Hospital in London through all the blitzes. I came to realize, as I had never done before, the loyalty and unity of our family and how much it had sustained me.

Then there was Kathleen. To me our relationship had grown, in the five years apart, into a central place in my life. It amazed me how our friendship had matured and deepened in the separation. From the first time we had met I had had a real interest in her. We saw each other from time to time at Queen's University and on holidays in Ballycastle, but little more. When I went off there was quite a low-key farewell.

Yet something had started, a seed had been sown. I can very clearly remember when I was en route for Egypt in 1940, debating if I should write to her. Then one day I started and I wrote sixteen pages of YMCA notepaper. I waited many weeks for a reply which arrived when I was in the desert. I must admit I was slightly disappointed when it did arrive and ended with just 'yours sincerely'. The following two ended with 'yours very sincerely' and 'yours most sincerely'. I could not decide if this marked any progress. At last one did arrive signed 'yours with love' and I knew that the Rubicon had been crossed.

What a strength and inspiration Kathleen's love was! It brought home to me just how important such a relationship can be, and how it transcended time and place. How right and proper for us to become engaged even before I returned home.

Yet the actual coming home was beyond description. That

agonizing week for Kathleen after the war had ended, and still no news. (Our Stalag was one of the last to get free.) Those halting phone calls to Edinburgh, and how speechless we both were. That overnight journey from Euston to Waverley station in Edinburgh and the arrival at 7:50 a.m. The meeting and how complete it was with no strain or uncertainty. How the years dropped away and we knew that we both had grown together even through the years apart, and all that had happened to each of us. I knew what she had meant to me in those past years and began to think of all we could do together in the years that lay ahead.

# CHAPTER FIVE

# *Vision*

*What would life be without its dreams?* NANSEN

*I will pour out my spirit on all flesh . . . your old men shall
dream dreams and your young men shall see visions.*
JOEL 2:28

Coming home after five such action-packed years was quite a
shock. It was not only the length of time but also the sudden
change from a regimented and institutionalized society. It had
also been all-male and, in addition, most decisions were made
by other people. What a jolt it was to move back into private life
again, where each had to make his own decisions and plan in
advance about the future. The adjustment did take quite a long
time. It was like wakening up again after an unpleasant dream.

I remember very clearly how unromantic my departure from
the army system was. We had arrived in our great Dakota troop-
carrier at an RAF base at Oakley in Kent. Here we were assembled
in a huge hangar with lines of tables laid out. We were very
graciously welcomed by the staff, and the process of finding out
details and receiving instructions began. Suddenly I realized
something that I had almost forgotten, that I was not a soldier
nor under military orders, nor did I need to be 'posted back' to
my unit and wait weeks or even months to be demobilized. So
very politely I lifted up my pack, explained to the officer-in-
charge who I was and that I was off to report to 'my unit in
London' – the National YMCA. Thus I took my departure from
the army and set off for the local railway station.

It was a very simple thing that made me realize that I was truly
free and at last on my own. When I arrived at the station I took
a train for London. There were very few passengers travelling
and in the compartment where I sat down I found two old ladies

talking together. One of them had been reading the *Daily Mail* and the other knitting a pair of socks. They were both so calm and sedate. How comfortable and soft the seats seemed to be and how smoothly the train glided along the rails. Outside, the countryside looked fresh and green with its hedges, trees, small fields, farmsteads and woodlands, in contrast to the drier and sparser land in Germany. The whole atmosphere was so genteel, quiet and normal, dispelling all pressures and anxieties about what lay ahead.

As I sat there and drank it all in I felt deeply moved, as somehow my feelings began to come back. A great deep profound sense of gratitude swept right through my whole being. I could not put it into my own words but recalled Siegfried Sassoon's lines:

> Everyone suddenly burst out singing;
> And I was filled with such delight
> As prisoned birds must find in freedom,
> Winging wildly across the white
> Orchards and dark-green fields; on-on-and out of sight
> . . . .
> My heart was shaken with tears; and horror
> Drifted away . . . O, But Everyone
> Was a bird; and the song was wordless; the singing
> will never be done.

It was like coming out of a very long tunnel into the clear bright air and returning to my own folk. I wrote very simply in my log:

> A lovely Dunmurry Sunday, the Lisburn Road buzzes with traffic, the old familiar noise as a train passes by the manse and whistles at the crossing, and though the crows in the trees caw as ever, all around there is a deep sense of peace and rest, with no further journeys to take or orders to obey. As I lie here in my old room bathed with the morning sun, I wish that

time would stand still so that I could drink it all in
again and again.

But as I looked out across the lawn and to the sandbank, where
we had played as children, and improvised so many ploys as
young adolescents, my joy was tempered and chastened. I
remembered several very close friends who would not come
home. So vividly I recalled the games we had played, and the
projects we had devised in and around the manse. One lost his
life in Burma, another at Gibraltar, and one other in the Western
Desert. What could I say to their parents? I could only be with
them. I will never forget the marvellous way they received me
in sharing my joy with no self-pity or bitterness. As I thought
about them, and so many others I had known, I began to ask
myself if there was not a better way to solve our national and
international quarrels and conflicts. Was there not a part I could
play in this during the rest of my life?

Soon the halcyon days of reunion and homecoming began to
pass, and I thought about the future and what role I should play,
and where I should play it. I must admit that it was a difficult
period and one that most people have to pass through at one
time or another in life. How should I decide what the next step
should be? I did in a sense envy those people who could say that
they had direct guidance to take up a particular career. But for
me and for most of us it does not come easily, and very often
involves a lot of searching and waiting. This means being open
and prepared for leads and opportunities that may come. I very
often quoted to myself John Addington Symonds' lines:

> We ask no dream, no prophet ecstasies,
> No sudden rending of the veil of clay,
> No angel visitant, no opening skies,
> But take the dimness of our souls away.

Two events did help me to come to terms with this new stage
of my life. First I was, at last, ordained by the Belfast Presbytery

in my father's church, just shortly before he retired. Then Kathleen and I were married in the church at Knock, where she had been brought up. Following this, I became assistant minister in McCracken Memorial Church in the suburbs of south Belfast. I spent seven happy months there, and it gave us both a breathing space in which to plan for the future. Kathleen had given up a teaching position in Ashleigh House, a Belfast girls' school, to train in youth leadership in Granton, near Edinburgh. I felt very strongly that I wanted to use the experience I had gained in the YMCA. We both were looking for something we could do in partnership.

Various opportunities came up, but we did not feel they were right for us. Then I met an old friend, Jimmie Haire, who was a professor in our theological college. He told me that the church authorities were going to appoint a full-time chaplain to my old university in Belfast, and I would be offered the job. This time I had no doubts. Here was a new and exciting challenge. It would be with young people, many of them just demobbed. This pioneering work would offer scope for experiments. Kathleen shared my enthusiasm. We really could work in partnership, and our past experiences would be most useful. Later on, in a whimsical mood I asked myself, 'Why have you been appointed to this work?' I had never claimed to be particularly academic. Was it because those who made the appointment believed that if I could survive three years in a prison camp, I could do the same in a modern university?

The mood of excitement and euphoria soon became subdued as I tried to come to terms with the job. I had no precedents or models on which to work. True I had a role, but I had to work it out by trial and error. I felt very much on my own at this point, as there were very few who could advise me. Much of my time was spent in drinking endless cups of coffee in the Students' Union and listening to those who would talk to me. At this stage the university seemed to be a very large and impersonal institution.

I eagerly welcomed an invitation from the Students' Christian

Movement to attend a conference for university chaplains in London. Perhaps here, I thought, I would get some help as to how I should operate. Alas, I was bitterly disappointed, not I should say with the programme or the other chaplains. Here I discovered that the structures of most English and Scottish universities were completely different from Queen's. Over the water the chaplaincies were built into, and financed by, the universities. Historical reasons made this impossible at Queen's. Chaplains were appointed and financed by the different churches and recognized by Queen's. This meant that they were very much on the periphery. This experience was very important for me. I saw that I had to work out a special model for Queen's. This had great advantages, as there were no traditions to hinder trying out new experiments. I began to think of all the war years. Had I been through those five years for nothing? I recalled those months in the YMCA in Tobruk. Was there anything there that could be used now? Could some of those ideas not be equally workable in the university setting? I remembered all I had learnt from Harold Barker. The YMCA had been a meeting place for multitudes of men under great pressure and in great need. It had been an open house for believers and unbelievers, those from different religious traditions and none, a place where the faith was affirmed and strengthened, where everyone who came, found encouragement and support. Why not try it out?

But how could this happen? I knew now that we needed a place where such ideas could be embodied. During these early days I was allowed, by the theological college authorities, to use one of the staff houses just behind the university for occasional meetings. Later I learnt that the house was to be sold. I knew that this was an opportunity that we could not miss. Money had to be found to buy the premises and put them in order. Fortunately we were able to get a grant from the church and 'Number Seven', as the students came to call it, was launched.

The Centre immediately caught on with the students. Much restoration was needed: walls painted, floors replaced and the garden put in order. The ensuing work-parties broke the ice and many who came to paint, stayed to discuss, study and to worship together. So also the social side, with hockey matches, a coffee bar and a very popular Saturday Night Club. Kathleen and I were able to have a flat in the building, and thus be available for any who wanted to drop in and talk. It was a very exciting time for both of us, as more and more students came. Here was a place that was open and with which they could identify. No attempt was made to indoctrinate or pressurize. We believed that participation was all-important in enabling those who came to know they were welcome and could contribute. In this way confidence and trust grew. The students felt accepted as they were and at their own level. We did all we could to help them to see that the Christian faith was not a limiting departmental activity for a few spiritually-minded, but rather a way of living that embraced all their activities.

I often felt inadequate at this time. There were so many different people with very different needs. I realized that I had been out of touch with university and church for five years and much had changed in this time, in the thinking and attitudes of young people. I was fortunate to find a small book which my father had been reading. It was called *We Shall Rebuild,* and the author was a very well known Church of Scotland minister, George MacLeod. It explained the key ideas behind his creation of the Iona Community. I had already heard him speak several times before the war and he impressed me deeply.

What immediately arrested my attention was that what he wrote fitted in with what I was feeling, but had not been able to work out. Experiences that had been important to me in the past, were here articulated and related to postwar life. First of all he reinforced and confirmed my experience of the Christian life as communal and about relationships between people. The Church was never meant to be a heterogeneous assortment of individuals, but a body of people bound together by their shared belief in the one God. 'The Bible', as MacLeod says, 'is about community: from the Garden of Eden to the city at the end.

From the family that in Eden fell, through the reconstituted Israel, its apex in Judah, its fellowship in the Acts and its expectation of ultimate peace round the Lamb that once was slain, the Bible is about community.' The other theme that 'rang a bell' with me was the central place he gave to the Incarnation. So much traditional nineteenth-century theology had tended to departmentalize the faith, and create a religious sector remote from the rest of life, and to suggest that the Christian Gospel has only to do with the spiritual. 'It is the perennial challenge to anyone who truly grasps the Incarnation – that God became man, that He clothed himself in the physical and thereby declared holiness to be inseparable from "material" considerations.'

These two insights provided me with an agenda not only for my personal faith, but also for work in the university. I had through the war years gained a fuller experience of the reality and presence of the Spirit of Christ and the urge to look beyond myself to other people and their needs. Now I began to see how this had to be worked out in this new environment.

George MacLeod makes this point in another of his books, *The One Way Left*. He explains how, in the gospels, Christ gives us three commands. First he tells us to **come** to him, to follow him in the discipline of our everyday lives. This commitment is basic and central. Second he tells us to **abide** in him. It is in our prayers and worship that we receive his 'bread for the journey'. We live in him as the branch lives in the vine. Thirdly he calls to **go** into the world to be his agents and presence there.

These then are the three parameters we tried to keep in mind as the Centre developed. Those years were very eventful and happy for us both. Our three children, Robert, Ian and Alison arrived and immeasurably enriched our lives. In fact they helped to create a homely and family atmosphere in the Centre, not only for those who dropped in, but mostly for those who shared the living accommodation in the house. This was specially true for those who came from outside Ireland.

We will never forget Immanuel. He came to Queen's from West

Africa. He was built like a middleweight boxer, but he had great difficulty in settling in to this new strange environment, and was very conscious of his colour. This meant that relationships were strained, he was very withdrawn, and at times aggressive and surly. But it was marvellous to see him with our children. He was completely transformed. He loved to talk to Ian, who was four years old. As he talked to Ian he was so gentle, relaxed and smiling. That was a turning point for him and he gradually found himself, and was able to go through his course, graduate and return home a mature and fulfilled person.

Kathleen also was able to play a full part in the ongoing life of the Centre. There were many visitors arriving who had to be entertained. In addition she was able to be a member of one of the many cells that developed to study different aspects of the faith relating to student life and the concerns of the outside world. We were very keen that the Centre should not be seen as a place of refuge from the university, but as the place where the students fulfilled their vocation. In our Forum meetings many university professors, including the Vice Chancellor, came to lead discussions on such subjects as Science and Religion, Medicine and Divine Healing, Faith and Politics. In one of his annual reports to the Senate Eric Ashby, the Vice Chancellor, wrote: 'There is no doubt that some of the students who have taken part in the life of this Centre will look back on their experience there as the most significant part of their university career.'

I soon recognized that student attitudes had changed. My pre-war generation had spent much time in debate, discussion and study groups. This new generation wanted to move beyond that to action and change. Many wanted the Church to be a 'creative minority' working for the underprivileged and the marginalized both at home and abroad. The speakers they wanted to listen to were those who were doing something. They flocked to listen to Trevor Huddleston from South Africa, George MacLeod of Iona and Tullio Vinay of Agape. They very much agreed with one of the visiting speakers, Bishop Stephen Neill, when he told them that the Christian needs to have three conversions: the first to Christ, the second to the Church and the third to the world.

The emergence of the Ecumenical Movement and the increasing desire for closer relationships between churches was growing in Ireland. Some of the students had been to international work camps run by the Youth Department of the World Council of Churches. Inevitably most of them came back full of enthusiasm to work for a wider vision of the Church. They began in the university organizing joint meetings and small groups to study the differences. Also a united carol service was planned and it included not only the different denominations but representatives of the whole university teaching and administration staff.

A frequent visitor, Mark Gibbs of Manchester, writer of the famous book *God's Frozen People* very eloquently and forcefully reminded us of the urgent need for the churches to recover the place and role of the laity. He believed that the task of the clergy is to service and resource the lay men and women in their front-line vocations in the world. Mark liked to quote Paul Johnston's words: 'The Church is too important to be left to the clergy.' He persuaded us to take very seriously 'the apostolate of the laity'. Of course the real question for us in Queen's was how could we make these ideas attractive and real to the students. It was not enough to identify the problems of the contemporary world, but also necessary to begin to deal with them. I saw that there was one thing I could do and that was to encourage our young people to use part of their summer vacation going to visit different countries, especially those with whom a few years earlier our country had been at war. So in the summer vacation of 1952 Kathleen and I set out with a group of twenty students to Italy. While we were fascinated to visit Rome and Florence, the real target was to spend five days living away up in the Christian youth village, called Agape, some 3000 feet up in the Cottian Alps, about thirty miles west of Turin. I had chanced to read about this centre and its leader Pastore Tullio Vinay in a magazine, and so we decided to go and find out what it was like and meet the organizers. That journey from Turin was one of the most exciting I have ever made. Our enthusiasm was tempered by the agony and ecstasy of the bus journeys. We had to change buses three times, as the spiralling roads got narrower and steeper. Whenever I looked out, there seemed to be no distance between the speeding wheels of our bus and a precipitous drop over the edge. So I just sat back and relaxed, comforting myself with a renewed belief in predestination. At last our bus drew up in the market square of the small village of Prali. Our arrival was a real event, as the villagers crowded around and our hosts from Agape greeted us and took our bags on their shoulders for a further climb of a kilometre to the place itself.

Of course we were exhausted after the long journey through the heat of the day, but exhilarated, as the outline of the village came into sight. I was surprised and impressed. It was built of solid brown and grey blocks of granite, and beautifully landscaped into a plateau on the mountainside. Our eyes were drawn to a striking campanile which set off and balanced the main hall and dormitories terracing up the slope of the mountain. How glad we were to sit down to rest, and gradually drink it all in, the crystal-clear air, the absolute stillness except for the distant tinkle of the cowbells as the cattle and sheep returned from their pasture in the hills. At first we were wondering if this delectable place was not an escape from the real world below. But we soon discovered how wide of the mark we were, when we listened to their story. They were indeed worthy representatives of their small Waldensian Church – the indigenous Protestant Church of Italy – whose history dates right back to the twelfth century. Their history is one of almost continuous martyrdom and persecution. Now these young men had just passed through the terrible ordeal of German occupation and ensuing civil war between the Fascists and the Partisans. This was the story they told me.

During the war Vinay had been the Waldensian pastor in Florence, where there was a large colony of Jews. When the

Germans occupied the city, the Gestapo proceeded with their infamous policy of extermination. Vinay is a man of great courage and compassion and when he discovered that the Jewish people had no rabbi, he knew that he had to act. He decided to organize an escape procedure, and through it he was able to assist many Jews to get away into the comparative safety of the countryside. This was very difficult, as all exits were carefully watched. He discovered that there was a considerable space between the floor of his flat and the ceiling of the church below. So he set to work and built a small room in the space, with a concealed trap door in the floor of his study. In this way he was able to hide Jewish families and assist them to escape from the city when the way was clear. Some sixty Jews were able to use this exit to safety. Small wonder that the Jewish community came to call him The Rabbi of Florence!

When the war finished he was appointed youth pastor for the North of Italy. He was a most appropriate person, as he had been in very close touch with a great number of young people during the ruthless civil war which had waged between the Fascists and the Partisans, many of whom were young Waldensians. Understandably after the war many of these young people were disillusioned by all they had experienced. Yet it was a group largely of these same people that had helped Vinay to build Agape. In their meeting together they had discovered afresh the Gospel message of healing and hope. This is how they described what they did: 'Amazed when we realized God's love for us, we determined to do something to show our gratitude. So we decided to carve out the face of Christ on the Alps.'

Agape was the sign of gratitude to God for the way they had been brought through such terrible times and a means of rediscovering the Hope of the Gospel for the future.

They were completely down-to-earth, and set about building Agape, the village of Christian love, 3,000 feet up in the Alps. They quarried the stone, mixed the cement and cut the wood. It was a demanding task, and soon young people in other countries heard about it and came to work with them to build this place of meeting where the barriers of race, class and colour were broken down as they worked together. On the day of the opening I Corinthians chapter 13 was read with its matchless description of the qualities of Christian love. So Agape (the Greek word for love) was born, and a vision of Christian Community and hope made real and living for the new generation.

This Italian trip gave us all much food for thought. One night towards the end of our stay I found that I could not sleep. I kept on thinking of our situation in Ireland: our divisions, the complacency of so much of our church life, and how so many social and political problems were ignored. Then I began to think of the young people at Agape: what so many of them had been through, and how they were attempting to face their problems in the light of the Gospel. Was there not something that we could do in Ireland? Could we have a meeting place where we might begin to work out our differences? At least here we had been given a vision of what could be done. Why not in Ireland?

This was confirmed for me within the next few days. On the way back to Ireland we had to break our journey at Basel in Switzerland. There we stayed at a 'Blaukreuz' House. In conversation with the Director, I casually asked if this was where the world-famous theologian, Professor Karl Barth, lived. He assured me that it was, and went on to ask if I would like to meet him. Almost before I could reply, he had made contact by phone with the great man himself. I briefly explained who we were. Then he asked how many were in the party, and when I replied that we were twenty, he thought for a moment and said that would be too many for his room, but he would come and see us. Soon he arrived. You may guess how I felt. Barth's name was a household word throughout the Christian world. He was described as the greatest theologian since Calvin. His theology had inspired the Confessing Church in Germany's great and costly resistance to the idolatry of Hitler and his eventual downfall. Now here he was, this outgoing man, with his dark greying hair, penetrating brown eyes, so relaxed as he lit his pipe and listened to us.

He at once put us at our ease by his humour and friendliness, asking about our trip and how things were in Ireland. He suggested that we might like to ask him questions. This continued for over an hour, until finally one Irish student asked: 'Sir, what can we do for world peace?'

Barth replied: 'Go home and set your own house in order.'

# CHAPTER SIX

# *Annunciations*

*The angels keep their ancient places;-*
*Turn but a stone, and start a wing!*
*'Tis ye, 'tis your estrangèd faces,*
*That miss the many-splendoured thing.*

*But when so sad thou canst not sadder*
*Cry – and upon thy so sore loss*
*Shall shine the traffic of Jacob's ladder*
*Pitched between heaven and Charing Cross.* FRANCIS THOMPSON

I used to think, as I imagine many others have done, that the
Spirit comes only to very special people like St Paul, St Francis
or John Wesley but not to ordinary people like us. Now, as I look
back over the Corrymeela years, I can understand what Jacob the
patriarch meant when, after his dream at Bethel, he exclaimed:
'Surely God is in this place and I was not aware of it.' So many
things have happened, so many little annunciations, that I
cannot but be conscious, in spite of all our dimness and
unawareness, that Someone infinitely great and wonderful has
been at work all the time, even in the tardy steps that we did take.

One of the first was in June 1965 when we had just completed
the purchase of the Corrymeela premises at Ballycastle. A group
of forty to fifty gathered in the lounge on a Saturday afternoon.
Our purpose was to express our gratitude to God, and to dedicate
ourselves and the newly occupied house to the work of Christian
reconciliation in Ireland. It was not a very impressive occasion
and we were a little self-conscious and unsure how it would turn
out. It was the first Corrymeela event and somehow had taken us
by surprise. Indeed the building itself was still being renovated
and was not fully functional. There were not even enough chairs
to go round and some had to stand. It seemed almost a non-event,

and yet a first step had been taken and something had happened. It made us understand in a new way that God does not always use the big spectacular events, but the ordinary material of everyday life.

In our worship the Scripture was taken from Luke and I focused on this passage: 'If you then, that are evil know how to give good gifts to your children, how much more will your Father, who is in heaven, give the Holy Spirit to those who ask him!' I used this passage in the short address which followed, because I wanted to assure myself and those present that God was really with us in this venture and that it was not just ourselves alone: 'God is saying just that to us today: "Have more faith in me, understand the sort of God I am. If you want a place where people can come together to know me better, where they can think about my world and my purpose for it, a place where my followers can be united, especially those from different parts of my broken body, and learn to trust each other; if you want that, I want it infinitely more." Let us try to see what he would have this place be, the role it can play in the life of this country, a place of training and meeting, of peace and renewal and of challenge and response.' Reflecting on that simple occasion today it is inspiring to see how our prayers were answered and our hopes fulfilled, although our faith was so tentative and small.

These lines of Janet Shepperson, a Corrymeela member and a poet, express perfectly what we all felt that day:

> I offer you this hope.
> It is so small
> the wind could blow it out.
> Its feeble flickering
> turns up in unexpected places
> and seems to annoy those
> with a big investment in dazzling light,
> or in measuring the strength of darkness.
> If this hope lives
> it will be like swallows' wings,

> erratic, unpredictable,
> always on the move.
> If this hope dies,
> It will be buried shallow
> like grass seed.

We were well aware that we had planted a seed that day and perhaps our worship was in keeping with a small and quiet act of faith.

Of course that June event did not just drop from the sky like a magic carpet. Much has happened since Agape in 1952. The Centre at Queen's was learning to look beyond itself and focus on concerns in the local situation and the outside world. The population explosion, race, and the bomb were very much on the agenda in the sixties. Relationships between the different churches were widely debated, and for many Christians there was a growing call to look afresh at the scandal of our divisions, and the damage it did to our Gospel message.

At the university visits by George MacLeod and other international figures helped to stretch our Irish horizons and encourage us to take an initiative in our static society. George's ever-recurring theme, on the rediscovery of Christian community, struck a chord in our thinking. John Morrow, later to become leader of Corrymeela, Alec'Watson and myself sent out invitations for an exploratory meeting. Some fifty turned up, Christians from all backgrounds. The group included housewives, trades and professional people as well as a number of interested students. The three of us realized very quickly that the others were most enthusiastic about the idea of a new community. This could counter the current apathy and complacency, and open up new possibilities. Of course when it came to concrete suggestions about the nature and location of the proposed community, it was difficult to find consensus. We knew that we had to take time so we continued to meet and pray together, that we should be shown the way.

Suddenly at a meeting early in 1965 someone very casually

informed the gathering that the Holiday Fellowship Centre near Ballycastle in County Antrim, was up for sale. That news immediately concentrated our thinking. No longer could we indulge in rather abstract discussions on the nature of Christian community. Now we had to face a real choice, and our ideas and visions were put to the test. I knew the Centre well as I had often been past it when on holiday at Ballycastle, and from the start was utterly convinced that this was the place for us. The others felt that we should at least investigate the possibilities and so a group was appointed to visit the Centre.

I went along with three others and we had a very positive visit to Corrymeela, and became excited about its possibilities. It was ideal for our plans, with its delectable setting right on the beautiful North Antrim coast. We were thrilled to see the excellent accommodation which might now be available for us. I immediately began to visualize the potential for children, young adults and older people. There was plenty of space and a large dining hall, lounge and conference room. In the grounds we explored twenty chalets, which could be used for additional groups. We also learned, to our delight, that the large field adjacent to the grounds would be available for sale. It seemed as though our dreams were beginning to materialize. Although much rehabilitation work was necessary, we could see that most of it would be within the range of voluntary labour. So in good heart we reported our findings to the next meeting, and it was unanimously agreed that we proceed with the purchase of the property. This was an act of faith as we had no funds, but we believed that together we could raise the money.

I immediately went to the estate agent and made an offer. He seemed quite convinced that we would get the site as no other offers had materialized. Even so the next weeks were anxious for me, and I phoned from time to time. Finally on the Friday of a holiday weekend I could stand it no longer. I went in person to the office and pressed the agent very strongly to accept our offer, which he finally did. I came home very excited with the prospects that began to open up for our embryonic community.

This excitement was somewhat tempered when I learned, later, that a representative of another interested party had arrived in the agent's office after the weekend, and offered a much more substantial amount for Corrymeela. To his everlasting credit the agent stuck to his verbal agreement and we now had our Centre! I am sure this was another little annunciation for us.

This was followed by many other little miracles. Soon we discovered that in our preoccupation with acquiring Corrymeela we had forgotten one crucial point: Who would be able to go and live there, someone who could look after it and begin to put the place in order? There was much that had to be done. We had never thought about that, and none of us was free to go. Then Billy McAllister came into the picture. He had attended some of the meetings, but said very little. Now as we were all feeling very deflated and anxious, he very modestly indicated that he would be free to go, if we could not get anyone else. As I think now of all he did, and all he gave us, I know that Billy was 'sent' to us, because I am sure that if we had been able to search the length and breadth of Ireland we could not have found a more suitable person. He brought all the practical skills which none of us had, from his experience as an engineer at Dundalk Railway Maintenance Depot. And how priceless they were, when there was so much work needed to repair and restore the premises. But far more important were his special gifts of relating to and accepting all sorts of people. Billy was an authentic community man, able to make those who came feel not only accepted and wanted, but also able to contribute themselves – be they skilled electricians or unskilled enthusiasts. Derick Wilson, one of the first students to come, described what Billy meant to him:

> Billy McAllister was a personal friend to me and to many many others, a father figure with his twinkling smile, a mischievous leprechaun who was dismayed when laughter and revelry stopped too early, and did not start soon enough . . . Billy, aged 'somewhere

between sixty and a lot more', was a gift to Corrymeela. To Corrymeela he offered the concept of a live presence, being the first person to stay there. This was not just to secure the building, but a hope for its future in its use and programme. The evolution of the Corrymeela Community, born out of the interest of so many students, always has been significant for me, in that the first person to live in Corrymeela was a tradesman, one who made his living by the skill of his hands. Images of Christ come to mind in the statement that Billy's presence there made. He demonstrated the care and precision of the carpenter, the importance of basic skills in making furniture and other essentials of home. He combined these skills with a daily discipline of prayer and Bible study, and a way of living with others that sought to find the Christ in them – most of the time – because Billy, like us all, was human.

Billy has now joined the cloud of unseen witnesses but I never climb up the winding road from McGuire's Strand to Corrymeela House without the sense that Billy's presence is still around the site, willing us on in our work.

The time came towards the end of 1965 when we knew that we had to go public and let the wider community know that we had started and what we were about. So on a blustery October Saturday we gathered with our friends and supporters, some two hundred in all, in the Corrymeela Lounge. We had come together to open the Centre as a place for Christian Reconciliation in Ireland. Among those who came there was a great mixture in age and tradition. It was a happy and relaxed day, beginning with the procession of work campers cheerfully wending their way up from the coast road. They were dressed in their jeans and T-shirts, and carried all the various tools they had used in the restoration of the House. They were a noisy and colourful procession, brandishing not only spades, shovels, picks and paint brushes, but also kettles, pots and pans, recognizing that everyone had a part to play.

The climax for us all was when Tullio Vinay, who had come from Agape to be with us, entered the conference room and declared Corrymeela open. The short speech he made, in broken but most effective English, has remained ever since as a continuous challenge to us.

> In this moment of deep emotion for me I wish that with the help of the Living Lord this centre may become:
>
> FIRST: a place of preaching the New World as we see it in the person of Jesus Christ. The world needs to see this message in the real world of men. Here, living together, the New World in work and prayer, you may point it to all categories of men and push them to the same research, be they politicians, economists, sociologists, technicians, workers or students.
>
> SECOND: a place of encounter and dialogue with all men; believers and unbelievers. The believers need the presence of the unbelievers, because they represent a criticism of our way and life; the unbelievers need us if we have real news to bring. A member of the Italian Parliament once said to me: 'I am not religious but I am terribly attracted to Christ.'
>
> THIRD: to be a question-mark to the Church everywhere in Europe, so that they may review their structures and tasks, and be free from this instinct of preservation, to hear the time of God for its mission in the world.
>
> FOURTH: more than all, that you – being together – have always open eyes and ears to understand when the Lord is passing nearby, to be ready to follow the way He shall indicate to you. As a Church we should not have an inferiority complex – not because we are

or have something – but because every possibility is given to us as His instruments.

In my response as leader I spoke of our vision for Corrymeela:

> We hope that Corrymeela will come to be known as 'the Open Village', open to all people of good will who are willing to meet each other, to learn from each other and work together for the good of all.
>
> Open also for all sorts of new ventures and experiments in fellowship, study and worship.
>
> Open to all sorts of people; from industry, the professions, agriculture and commerce.
>
> This is part of our vision. We know we are only at the beginning and there is so much to be done.

For me personally Tullio Vinay's presence and words were most moving and inspiring. As I heard him speak I thought of all he had been through and all he had done. I remembered the Agape Centre, and now we had one in Ireland. It was also for me a healing of memory as I thought of those grim months in Italian prison camps, and all that we had suffered. Here was the real voice of Italy giving us a vision of how the 'New World of Jesus Christ' might begin here in this place.

Very soon the excitement and euphoria passed, as we came to realize what we had undertaken, and how much had to be done. Quickly our structure, which had been very loose, was formalized. A council was elected, my appointment as leader was confirmed and a treasurer and secretary elected, all on a voluntary basis. Indeed at that stage the only staff who were employed were non-resident domestic workers from Ballycastle. Billy McAllister became honorary Resident Warden. The survival and development of the community was due mainly to the voluntary efforts of a large group of lay people who gave unstintingly of their time, skill and energy. There is truth in the phrase: 'Behind every visionary there must be a treasurer.' Only to that, in our case, must be added lawyers, architects, engineers, doctors, housewives, cooks and many other unsung heroes. Then as the programme got under way teachers, youth and community workers advised on appropriate programmes, and encouraged young people to come and participate. Many others organized fund-raising events and went round churches, schools and clubs telling about this new adventure. All the early programmes were planned and carried through by Community members. I think specially of the summer Family Weeks. These ran through July and August and were planned and staffed by Community members for those who could never afford a holiday.

So the voluntary principle was, and still is, a very important element in Corrymeela. Each member commits himself or herself to play a part in giving time, as well as financial support and prayer, to the work. This has remained very central for us, although, as the range and outreach increased, full-time professional staff have been needed. But the main thrust and vitality lies with the membership. Often this has been an area of tension, between the trained and untrained, the professional and the volunteer. It is, I believe, a creative tension, as it is recognized and frequently debated. It also provides a safeguard against institutionalism and bureaucracy. So the survival of this fragile experiment has been due to the work and dedication of a large number of lay people. In addition to my role at Corrymeela I was still chaplain with Desney Cromey, my colleague, in Queen's University. This meant that we were in daily touch with a large number of students and graduates, and able to encourage them to take part in the work camps during the summer vacation. It would be difficult to exaggerate the importance of this for the evolution of our community. From these groups many of the future members and leaders emerged. In addition, the work they were able to do was most necessary for our survival, as we did not have the money to employ professional labour at this early stage. So week after week during the summer, teams of young people turned up. They came to paint, clean, repair and cook;

to dig trenches for drainage, water pipes and electric cables; to cut wood, mix cement and lay foundations. In fact, to be a work camper was to be ready for anything. Desney Cromey, the first co-ordinator, describes the initial welcome for a new recruit:

'Come in and make yourself at home – it is good to have you here.' This would be followed by instructions: 'The first thing you have got to do is to make your bed.' A little taken aback, the new arrival would ask: 'Where are the blankets and sheets?' Desney's smiling response would be: 'Well, here is some wood, go and ask Billy for a hammer and nails.'

There were other things ultimately far more important than the work – notably the personal development, self-understanding and discovery of faith that took place in these weeks for many of the participants. This is part of what I wrote at the time:

> The work camp helps to express the idealism, the desire to do something worthwhile for others, which is characteristic of many of this generation. The work experience is unifying, inspiring, and, in the deepest sense, a spiritual one. It provides a common ground on which all types can meet: the articulate and inarticulate, the extrovert and the introvert, the mature and immature. In communal work no one can dominate or steal the show. Everyone is able to contribute, and the shared tasks create the confidence, unity and trust of a true family. In this atmosphere discussion of the deepest questions is easy and the simple worship at the end of each day natural and real.

As I write, a vivid picture flashes into my mind. The work campers were repainting the outside of the Main House. This entailed the use of very tall forty foot ladders as the high end gables were tackled. Two of these ladders were set side by side, and at the top of one was Billy McAllister busy with his brush.

Alongside him at the top of the other ladder was Dave, a nineteen-year-old student. While he was keen to work, he described himself as an agnostic with little interest in religion. There was quite a keen wind blowing in off the sea and the ladders swayed with it. Both painters were oblivious to this, and while they were busy at the painting, they were also absorbed in a deep theological discussion. With the wind blowing it was only possible to hear the odd snatch of their dialogue. Dave was asking Billy some leading questions, and the one that was overheard was: 'Billy, do you really believe that there is life after death?' Surely it was the right time and place to raise such a question!

Corrymeela began in 1965, several years before the violence broke out in 1968/9. We could see all too clearly, even when we started, that our little country was deeply divided. At the university the unrest, the antagonism to the status quo and the polarization were rapidly increasing. As a chaplain I was very closely in touch with what was happening. Discord and violence were escalating. The university was right at the centre and at the start was the focal point of the opposition. A large number of the students came from a strongly Nationalist background. They believed that as the minority they had been unjustly treated by the government, and their people had suffered discrimination in housing and employment, and in general they had been looked on as second-class citizens. Attempts at redress and change had been initiated, but progress was slow. So the call to violent methods was beginning to attract many from the Nationalist community.

Soon it became clear to the students at the university that a choice was opening up. For the Nationalist the choice was between pursuing a peaceful way of working for change, or getting involved in violence and 'the armed struggle'. For the student from a Unionist background the choice again was either to follow a peaceful process for change or, as many did, just to 'opt out' and live a private life. Very quickly we began to grasp the importance of our existence as an alternative to violence and to apathy, by offering the way of co-operation between the two traditions, and also to recall and reaffirm the Christian values of justice and peace, and the dynamic of the Gospel of forgiveness, to which the vast majority of students of both traditions gave at least lip service. Our task was to try, even in a small way, to make this alternative visible.

This was a very tense and challenging time for us. We asked ourselves if there was something we could do, or did we just wait and hope for the best? We believed that we now faced our first real test. Were we really in earnest? How could we make this known? Should we not move right into the public domain? Most of us were not politically sophisticated, but we had some good friends who were, and they encouraged us to take an initiative, so with their help we planned 'Community 1966 – a joint Protestant and Roman Catholic Conference'. This was a unique event at such a time.

We were greatly heartened when the Prime Minister, Captain Terence O'Neill, agreed to give the keynote address on our theme. Community leaders and politicians from both sides agreed to be present. Also we went for the fiftieth anniversary of one of the most emotive events in the history of this country, the Easter Rising of 1916. In addition it was the anniversary of the Battle of the Somme, in which many thousands of Ulstermen had lost their lives.

It was with a mixed sense of excitement and apprehension that I approached Friday 8th April. There were so many things to think about, as this was the first major gathering in Corrymeela. We were still putting down carpets an hour before the Prime Minister was due to arrive. A large party of police turned up to provide security, not only from possible IRA attacks, but also from Protestant Loyalists who deplored the idea of such a joint meeting. We were greatly relieved when the weather came to our aid and a night of strong wind and continual blustery rain provided a great deterrent to any would-be opposition.

It was with feelings of relief and elation that we watched the last guest depart. The key speech by the Prime Minister was acknowledged to be one of the best and most positive he ever gave. This is the appeal with which he ended:

> If we cannot be united in all things, let us be united in working together in a Christian spirit to create better opportunities for our children, whether they be from the Falls Road or from Finaghy. In the enlightenment of education, in the dignity of work, in the security of home and family, there are aims which all of us can pursue. As we advance to meet the promise of the future, let us shed the burdens of traditional grievances and ancient resentments. There is much we can do together. It must and – God willing – it will be done.

This speech and the meeting itself dominated the news media after the weekend. So Corrymeela was well and truly launched and as the leading article in the Belfast Telegraph commented: 'Through Captain O'Neill and those who organized the community conference, Corrymeela takes its place in Irish history.'

CHAPTER SEVEN

# *A Place of Refuge*

*To an open house in the evening*
*Home shall men come,*
*To an older place than Eden*
*And a taller town than Rome.*
*To the end of the way of the wandering star,*
*To the things that cannot be and are,*
*To the place that God was homeless*
*Now all men are at home.* G.K. CHESTERTON

One of the first questions asked at the Centre is about the meaning of the word 'Corrymeela'. It is an Irish word and has several interpretations. Recently a visitor from Scotland told me that it could mean 'a place of refuge'. Indeed local historians have suggested that within the present grounds there is such a place. It is identified as the compact little mound seen on the left hand side as you walk up from the coastal road and McGuire's Strand to the Centre. The location is right on the edge of the cliff and makes an ideal position of security, with a deep drop on all sides except for a wide grass corridor as a bridge to the roadway. Such places of refuge were common in the Celtic period, with its numerous duns, forts, crannogs and round towers.

It is sobering to realize that still in our twentieth century such places are necessary. From very early on this same role has been very central in Corrymeela's history. From 1968 the political situation began to deteriorate, as the O'Neill reforms not only failed to satisfy the minority, but also his concessions alienated his supporters. Eventually he was replaced and Brian Faulkner took over, the army was called in and six months later, on 9th August 1971, Internment was declared. This immediately resulted in very serious unrest and violence. The death toll escalated and very fierce fighting broke out in many parts of the country between the security forces and the paramilitaries. This sparked off much rioting and intimidation in mixed areas. Slogans such as: 'Get out or be burnt out' appeared and petrol bomb attacks were made not only against the police and army but also homes, shops and factories. There was widespread looting and life became very hazardous, especially for families. Many people, in their desperation, took whatever transport they could get and set off for Dublin and the Republic.

One of our young members, Liz Parkin, working on a summer programme in Ballymurphy, a large and run-down housing estate in West Belfast and strongly Nationalist, phoned me in Ballycastle and pleaded that Corrymeela should be used to accommodate some of the families now at risk. I replied that we would come up immediately with the minibus, the only one we had, and start to evacuate the families, and asked her to make the necessary plans.

It was for us at Ballycastle a relief to learn that there was something that we could do. It had been so frustrating to listen hour by hour to the news and learn of the distress of so many people, and be powerless to do anything about it. Now our agenda was set. I departed for Belfast with Gilbert, one of the summer staff. We approached the city from the south-west, via Dundrod, and as we were crossing the Antrim hills above the city an army vehicle stopped us. The officer asked us where we were going and we told him. He warned us that there was no way through and that it was dangerous. I suggested that it would not be dangerous for us, and eventually he allowed us to continue. Next we began the long descent down the Upper Springfield Road. There was no other traffic in sight, and we had an eerie feeling of uncertainty.

Next, just as we came round a long bend, a priest appeared and waved us down with a handkerchief. Apparently he expected us, as he quickly explained that this road was blocked, but if we could go back for about half a mile, we could get down on to the Glen Road, and there the children would come to meet us. Soon we dropped down to the lower road, but had not travelled far when we were halted again. A huge lorry had been parked right across the road and there was no way through. We stopped at a discreet distance, as we could see several people at the lorry. One of them, a middle-aged man, apparently the owner of the vehicle, was arguing with two young adults. They seemed to be making preparations to set the lorry on fire, and use it to block the road. We were close enough to hear the exchanges between them. The owner was obviously very upset at the prospect of losing his lorry. He told the two youths in no uncertain terms that he was as good a Republican as they were. We were getting worried at this point in case they decided to use our minibus as a substitute for the lorry. Fortunately at this point a group of children came walking past the doomed lorry and rushing over to us immediately piled into the bus and quickly we were on our way in the other direction. This journey we made very frequently over the next weeks as the fear and uncertainty increased. More and more children with a few parents began to arrive at Ballycastle. We quickly decided that we had to get more accommodation as Corrymeela was already very fully occupied with the regular summer programme. So we turned to the local schools. I went to see the headmaster of the High School and explained our predicament. His response was magnificent: 'I should of course call a Governors' Meeting and get permission to do this. But here are the keys of the school including the kitchens and the gymnasium.'

Within three hours we were operative. The school catering staff volunteered to man the kitchens. Mattresses and blankets were available as a music summer school had just ended. Forty Corrymeela volunteers arrived in a few hours and undertook the supervision of the children. The Cross and Passion Convent and St Patrick's Primary school also helped with accommodation. Many of the local shopkeepers, both Catholic and Protestant, donated clothes and footwear as well as food and toys. Now the town knew what Corrymeela was about and that we meant what we said.

This is the story of one of the mothers, Margaret Mulvenna,

and her young family of seven children. They lived in the Turf Lodge estate on the outskirts of Belfast and off the Upper Springfield Road. Since the outbreak of violence, life had been very difficult in the estate with hijacking of vehicles, petrol bombing and much shooting. This was Margaret's description of what happened:

On the morning of Internment, 9th August 1971, we were awakened out of our beds by squealing and yelling and the sound of army Saracens driving round the streets. Men and boys were dragged from their beds and taken away. It was an awful experience to come through and it made me feel very bitter towards the soldiers and I knew my eldest daughter and two eldest sons felt exactly the same way. Only for the Grace of God and my maternal instinct to protect my family at all cost, we too could be a part of the violence which exists in Northern Ireland today. For two days and nights we lay on the floor in our sitting room, we could not go to bed, as the IRA and the British soldiers were in a non-stop gun fight.

On the third morning, at about 6:30 a.m., the shooting stopped. I went to the front door and saw the soldiers had surrounded the estate, and the shooting was over for a while. We gathered what clothes and food we could and we walked out of that estate. No one was allowed to go in or out. I shall never forget the commanding officer's face as I got to the road block with my seven children all clutching each other's hands. He just looked at us and the tears ran down his face as he commanded his men to let us through.

We made our way to a school about half a mile away and I was told there was a bus leaving Belfast. We all got into the bus. I did not know where it was going but I was so glad to get away I didn't care. This I would say, thank God, was the turning point of my life, this journey was to lead me to a people I didn't know existed, a people who cared and until the day I die I shall never be able to thank those people enough. The bus arrived at a little seaside town on the very north of Ireland. It was called Ballycastle and as I was stepping out of the bus a tall gentle-looking man took my hand to help me. His words will always be implanted in my mind; they were: 'You will be all right now.' I do not think he even knew the comfort and strength I got from those six words. For four years I had been on my own in the world, but since that meeting I have never been alone.

I will never forget the kindness we received in those difficult days, the meals that were provided for us in the school canteen, the sleeping quarters in the gym and how the students looked after the children, organizing games and taking them down to the shore and sand. That first stay in Ballycastle was a turning point in our lives. I believe, although I am a devout Catholic, it was my first real experience of Christianity. From then on I began to live and think reconciliation. I became a member of the Community four years later. Corrymeela involvement is the one thing in my life I shall always be grateful for. Many times my children and I could have been caught up in the turmoil and bitterness brought on by years of unrest, such as tragic deaths, army harassment and the Hunger Strike. But thanks be to God with the help of the Corrymeela Community and the prayers and support of other members, we have remained true to our commitment to work for peace and justice till this day.

This experience with Margaret and her family and many others like it were very important for us and our fledgling Community.

It gave us our identity and it helped us to demonstrate to a divided community that Christian compassion knows no barriers. This action left its mark and helped the people in the area and through the country to see that we did really mean what we said. Most of those who were helped were Catholic while, at this early stage, the Corrymeela members were Protestants. Dervla Murphy in her book *A Place Apart* makes this point in describing one woman she visited. Aine had just returned from Corrymeela where she had gone after the murder of her son. Dervla explained how Aine had greeted her and apologized for her red eyes, as she had not been expecting a caller:

> I was just having a wee cry in the kitchen. Mostly now I'm all right but sometimes it comes over me round this time – when he'd be comin' in for his supper with his dad. They worked together at the plumbin', see. And you know how a lad likes his food – he'd say, 'Great, Mum! It's onions tonight and you've been cryin!' People say that I will forget all these details but how can I? It was Corrymeela got me where I am now. I would never have come to myself without it. I never felt at Mass what I felt at those prayers together in Corrymeela. Protestants and Catholics we were, all together, and the Protestants knew 'twas theirs killed my son and they prayed special for me – and it worked! I'll never be happy again, see. But I'm not angry no more.

Again it was important for us as individuals and as a group to be brought face to face with the grim stark reality of what was happening to many of our fellow citizens in our cities and towns. Here we experienced the naked face of sectarianism: its driving demonic hatred and fear, its ruthlessness against any who resist it, its effects on families and children, its manipulation and intimidation of young adults and its tragic legacy of pain, sorrow and loss on innocent victims. Now all sorts of people began to arrive seeking the respite and safety of Corrymeela. No longer could we talk objectively about the activities of the paramilitary organizations, because a young man who had been 'done over' by them arrived in our midst in order to get away from them. We talked to him over several days as he tried to get back to some sort of normal life again. One could see something of what had happened to his body, but what about the scars that had been left on his mind and imagination, as he tried to work through and come to terms with what had happened to him?

On another occasion we had a family of five boys to stay for several days. Some months before, their father had been shot dead in crossfire in West Belfast when he had been assisting a mortally wounded priest, Father Mullan, who was trying to be a peacemaker. Just a few days before they came to Corrymeela one of them with his twin brother was lifted by the IRA and taken to a quiet place on the outskirts of the city. There one of them was shot because 'he had seen too much' and therefore might talk about what he had seen. The other was given his bus fare and told to go home. There was a great public outcry about this at the time and a group of priests published a statement expressing their disgust and outrage at such a deed. What could we say to comfort these young boys?

All we could do was to let them have time at Corrymeela to come to terms with what had happened and give them what support and encouragement we could. We promised that we would visit them in their homes. Even that, small as it was, was important and they still keep in touch and come to see us at Corrymeela from time to time. They have never forgotten what it meant to them in their time of need.

Every family, indeed every individual who came to Corrymeela brought a different experience as well as a different need. As I write, Peg Healy and her three boys come to mind, and what they have gone through since the Troubles began.

They first came to Corrymeela in the summer of 1972. Just a year before, on 9th August, 1971, Peg's son of almost fifteen years had been shot by British troops in one of Belfast's housing estates. That was the day of Internment and there had been fierce rioting and fighting all over the city and Desmond Healy had been one of the victims.

At the inquest the army claimed that he had been about to throw a petrol bomb. After warnings, an order was given and he was shot at once in the chest. But another witness later claimed that Desmond Healy was coming back from shopping and was carrying a bottle of sauce. The jury returned an open verdict. This is how Peg described her feelings:

> I just did not dare to believe that Desmond was dead. I could not accept it at first. Then when I began to realize what had happened a terrible hatred welled up in me. My son Michael went wild. He wanted to kill all around him. I had an awful job preventing him from joining some organization. All he wanted was revenge. Give Michael a gun and he would have murdered everybody.
>
> I could not even pass soldiers in the street without shouting at them. When I heard the news that soldiers had been killed I did not care how many were lying dead. I thought 'maybe that's the one that shot my child'. I didn't even care about their mothers. It was their fault for letting them come to Ireland. I just looked at the soldiers as animals. God, how I hated them.
>
> About a year after the boy's death the Legion of Mary send us to Corrymeela. I think Corrymeela was the first thing that brought Ted (Desmond's twin) to realize that he had to live, because before that he wouldn't have gone anywhere. He just didn't seem to want to mix with anybody at all. It was the best thing that ever happened, because it took him out of himself. He met people from all parts of the world. He made friends even, and he is good with children. And Corrymeela helped him to find a steady job.

Corrymeela is so homely. The housekeeper, Anna Glass, is very nice and she was good to us. And others too.

Going to Corrymeela helped my younger son, Michael. He really showed his brother's death. He was ready to knife the soldiers, throw stones and everything else. I didn't know what was going to happen to him. I was afraid to let him through the front door. He had this thing about Protestants, they were as bad as the army. He would not trust anybody but Catholics. But Corrymeela did help him. There he realized that all Protestants were not bad and all Catholics were not good. Corrymeela made a terrific difference to him. I think it also helped me. I still go to Mass but I have not taken the Sacraments, except once, since the boy died. A priest in the chapel said, 'If you can't forgive your enemy there is no point in taking Communion.' Well, I couldn't forgive. One priest I really liked said, 'God does not expect you to forgive suddenly. It will come.' He asked me if I wanted to take Communion and I did, the next morning. Later on the priest was transferred to another position and I have not taken the Sacraments since.

One day at Corrymeela I remember coming back to my room and I found the bedclothes in tatters and my own clothes all torn. Somebody had written 'Fenian bastards'. I was ready to go home. I felt everyone was against me. The leaders were terribly upset. They turned over everything to find out who had done it and they talked me into staying.

About four days later I was told who did it. It was a wee boy whose father and mother had abandoned him, and he was with a bunch of orphans at Corrymeela. I realized that he was not bad, only jealous of Michael and Danny because they had a mother. He really was looking for a bit of love. After that he came to me every night, and I took him on my knee. Maybe I learnt something from that.

It was Ray Davey, the leader of the Corrymeela Community, who made the difference about the soldiers. It was just the way he talked and listened. I'm still not too much in love with soldiers, but I suppose you have to try to stop hating. I began to think of the soldiers' mothers, or their wives or children; a life is a life. Maybe some of them have been through what I've been through.

It is only lately that I stop myself from shouting at them in the street. I still don't like them, but now I turn my back to them. I don't know about this thing forgiveness. But I do know that Corrymeela helped me and it helped Michael and Danny and Ted. I don't know how it will go in the end, but I suppose we'll have to live together no matter what way it goes . . .

Being a place of refuge was a very early phase in Corrymeela's history and it continues very central as still many need the sort of security we have described. Those who come are always given time and space to be on their own, if they want to, or to talk about what they have been through to someone who will listen and perhaps can help them to come to terms with what has happened. There is worship each day and they are free to attend if they want to. There is no pressure. Their particular needs will have a place in the prayers of the day.

This supporting, listening, caring role is a vital part of the continuing work of Corrymeela. It is here its depth is put to the test. It is this quiet ongoing awareness, prayer and action incarnated in the supporters, friends and members that keep Corrymeela alive. This need stretches far beyond those who have to face physical violence. There are so many other things that threaten our wider community: unemployment and loss of hope, broken relationships and bereavement, with fear, bigotry and despair. These are all part of the ongoing story of Corrymeela and its limitless agenda.

These early events and the variety of people who came, helped us at Corrymeela to come of age, to test out our vision and our courage. At the same time they did send out a signal to the wider community that we meant what we said and were determined to break through the sectarian barriers in whatever way we could.

One of our early visitors was the late Father Frank Culhane. He was a Holy Ghost Father from Dublin, but at that time had a parish in Switzerland. This is what he said in a broadcast from Lausanne after a visit to Corrymeela in July 1972:

> It is one of those places in which you find God in a special way because you are looking for Him in someone very different from yourself and your own tradition . . . I met, on leaving the house, six young children coming up the road. Their father had been killed in the Troubles a short time before. Their mother needed urgent hospital treatment, and it was Corrymeela that received these little victims of our politico-sectarian strife. Catholic orphans being cared for by young Protestant girls: a witness that our divisions are senseless and that if we are divided Christ is not.

CHAPTER EIGHT

# *Conflict*

To understand the past is to cease to live in it and to cease to live
in it is to take the earliest steps towards shaping what is to come
from the material of the present. F.S.L. LYONS,
THE TWO TRADITIONS BOOKLET

Saturday 19th March 1988 is a day that I will never forget. It was
late afternoon and a group of us were gathered in the Croi (This
is the Gaelic word meaning 'heart', so it is the place where
everyone in Corrymeela comes to meet, to celebrate and to pray.)
We were rehearsing for the BBC Sunday morning programme
*This Is the Day*, to go out next morning at 9:15 a.m. Our theme
was 'Blessed are the Peacemakers'. It was tedious work arranging
and timing the script with the various readings, music, prayers
and numerous repeats. The Croi was untidy, with three cameras,
seemingly dozens of technicians and microphones, wires and
pieces of equipment strewn all around. The powerful arc lights
had made the small space quite hot and stuffy.

During one of the many pauses I sat down for a brief rest, and
my attention was immediately drawn to a small monitor TV set.
It was switched on but without sound. A news flash was just
coming through about an incident at a funeral in Andersonstown
in West Belfast. I could see two soldiers in plain clothes in a car.
They were surrounded by a very hostile crowd, who were trying
to break the car and lay hands on the men. They were using
improvised weapons to break into the car and get at the men.
Some of them had large pieces of wood, others steel bars, and
one had a wheel-brace. Even without the sound it was terrifying
to watch. The flash ended and we were called back to the
rehearsal. I did not realize exactly what it was about, but I could
see that it was something horrific.

It was not until much later when I was going to bed, and was listening to the Northern Ireland News, that I learned the grim details about what had actually happened, and how the two soldiers had been attacked by the mourners attending the funeral of the three men who on the previous Wednesday, 16th March, had been callously assassinated by the Protestant loyalist, Michael Stone. These three had themselves been attending the funerals of the Provisional IRA members, Mairead Farrell, Daniel McCann and Sean Savage, who had been shot on March 6th by the SAS on the streets of Gibraltar while engaged in, it is believed, reconnaissance for a bombing mission.

I went to bed, but I could not sleep. I pondered again and again these terrible events so near at hand in Belfast. Milltown Cemetery is not more than half a mile from my home. We, Corrymeela, a community dedicated to peace and reconciliation, were to go on a live national TV programme in a few hours. Our theme was about peacemakers. I quickly realized that what we had prepared was already quite out of date given the ferocity of what had happened a few miles away. But what were we to say? Suddenly I felt weak and powerless and utterly inadequate. And yet as I thought and agonized about it, the answer came: 'If you as Christian peacemakers have nothing to say at a time like this, who has?'

When I came down to join the others at breakfast about 7 a.m. I said to the producer, Father Jim Skelly, 'Jim, I could not sleep last night.' He replied 'Neither could I.' Then together we went over the script and made some changes. I remember specially the prayer of confession. This we cut out, and instead the camera silently focused on the Coventry Cross of Nails which was on the wall. The silence lasted several moments. At the conclusion I just said: 'Father forgive', recalling Jesus' words from the cross and so acknowledging this present evil to be our responsibility as we all felt guilty and involved.

For some of us these terrible events were the most traumatic and harrowing to date. Among Community members there were very strong feelings and diverse interpretations as to what had happened.

But here in this service we all became very conscious of a profound sense of unity and mutual support as we, Catholics and Protestants in Corrymeela, witnessed together to our one Lord, who even at such a time held us together. I will never forget the quiet smile on the face of one of our young adults, Barry O'Hara. He was saying in his own way, 'This service is right, it is the only way – nothing can divide us – we all follow the one Christ.'

Those three shattering events in such close sequence reawakened us to the grim reality of our divided society. How deep the division was, and how real the hatred and fear, and how seemingly insoluble the conflict! It is all too easy to evade the issue by describing those involved as extremists who on both sides believe that the only way to bring about change is by violence. They may be a small minority, but they are able to operate because the rest of us have found no lasting solution to the conflict and, for the most part, have made little or no effort to do so.

I often quote the words of the Scottish theologian John McQuarrie: 'Violence occurs where conflict, which is not necessarily in itself a bad thing, has escalated to a point at which the conflicting parties no longer communicate with each other and seek only to coerce one another.' The first step is to recognize that there is a genuine conflict here and not to be sidetracked by the simplifiers who blandly affirm that it is entirely a security problem. On the contrary both sides have a real case. Winston Churchill in writing about Ireland many decades ago used the phrase 'the integrity of the struggle'. Both sides have a real case and a real solution must be found that will do justice to both. If this is to begin to happen we have to understand the background to the conflict.

It is only as we grasp something of the past history of Ireland that we can grapple with today's events. It is a long, long story but the seminal events that affect us today happened in the seventeenth century. The Plantation of Ulster by Scottish and to a lesser extent English settlers began in the early days of the century. It was James I's attempt to solve the problem of how to keep the Irish under control. Although the conquest of Ireland had taken place in the twelfth century rebellions and unrest continued. This new strategy of the Crown was to offer great tracts of land in Ulster to 'undertakers' in Scotland and England. In exchange for the land the Planters were committed to bring over skilled farmers, artificers and cottagers, who would settle on the land with their families. In this way it was hoped that a strong stable community would develop with its appropriate social and economic structures, in terms of schools, churches and local government.

At first the land was to be shared with the Irish inhabitants, but the Flight of the Earls out of Ireland was interpreted as treason, and from then on the land was just taken over, and the Irish driven off to the poorer parts and the hillsides. (The Flight of the Earls in 1607 led to the plantation of Ulster in 1608. It was alleged that they were plotting treason, so they thought it best to escape to the continent. As a result their lands were forfeited and given to settlers from Scotland and England.) This plantation method was very common at that time and it seems that similar plans to those used in Ulster were implemented in Virginia across the Atlantic.

One of the crucial flaws in this scheme was that it was only implemented in part. In spite of their promises the Scottish undertakers were just not able to get enough skilled people to come with them. The result was that much of the land was retained by the Irish. This fact did not diminish the hostility and resentment of the native people, and at the same time left a permanent mark of insecurity among the settlers. Thus was born the 'siege mentality' which is still deeply embedded in the settlers' racial memory and psyche. This was confirmed by the widespread Rising in 1641 when multitudes of the settlers were slaughtered across the country. The memory of 1641 is still part of Ulster folklore in certain parts of the province, and has been passed down from generation to generation.

The division of Ireland after the Anglo-Irish War and the Civil

War in Ireland led to the setting up of the Irish Free State made up of twenty-six counties and the establishment of the six Northern counties as a part of the United Kingdom but having its own government at Stormont in Belfast. Even these events did little to assuage the sense of insecurity in the minds of most Ulstermen. Perhaps it even intensified it as well as concentrating it in the North, because they realized that now the North was the main target of those who aimed at a united Ireland. A glance at many of the wall murals, the graffiti as well as the banners paraded on the Orange Marches on the Twelfth of July confirm this deep sense of anxiety. There is much emphasis on the symbols of defence and many affirmations about the permanence of its status as part of the United Kingdom. Thus we have 'Ulster is British', 'No surrender', 'Not an inch', 'What we have we hold', 'God save Ulster.'

These lead us on to the main elements of the conflict which have been there from the Plantation days. It is the all-important point that both religion and politics coincide and reinforce each other. Thus a majority of the Planters were Scottish Calvinistic Presbyterians while the Gaels were conservative Roman Catholics. So to this day political and religious difference aggravate and intensify the sense of separateness and threat. So events both outside and inside Ireland in the seventeenth century provided an agenda which is still unfinished and holds the country in its grip.

With the Tudors, the Reformation had taken over in England. The crisis began when James II came to the throne. Being an ardent Catholic he set out to reverse the policies of his predecessors and restore the power of the Roman Catholic Church. The result was that he had to take refuge in France, while the Protestant Prince of Holland William III, and his wife Mary, daughter of James, were crowned. James, with the backing of Louis XIV of France, launched a 'comeback' campaign in Ireland, where there was much support from the Catholic population.

William's victorious campaign in Ireland against James in the campaign of 1688–90 became immortalized in Protestant memory. This for them was how the history of the future was to be interpreted. God had saved his beleaguered people in their supreme hour of need. God's favour was believed to have fallen upon Protestantism. A walk through certain parts of Belfast and many other parts of Northern Ireland on anniversary occasions will make clear how deep these events lie in the psyche of many citizens. Every stage of William's campaign of deliverance from the shackles of Rome is faithfully chronicled and dramatized. The liberation of the besieged citizens of Derry in 1688, the famous victory at the Boyne in 1690, when James was routed, and the other battles at Aughrim and Enniskillen were treated as final events that set the pattern of Irish history for the future. The murals and the banners seem like those figures in ancient Greek sculpture, caught and frozen in their immortal struggle, unchanged by time and circumstance. In attempting to understand events so far back, it is important to realize the widespread fear and distrust other European powers had of Louis and his political ambitions. Indeed the Pope himself, Leo XI, was so suspicious of his intentions that he actually blessed King William's campaign against James and his French allies in Ireland. Yet those ancient fears of the seventeenth century still live on. They are kept alive by the power of the rhetoric, the colour and drama of the annual marches and festivals, but above all, by the ringing ballads and tunes:

The time has scarce gone by boys, two hundred years ago,
When Rebels on old Derry's Walls their faces dared to
    show,
When James and all his rebel band came up to Bishop's
    Gate;
With heart and hand and sword and shield we caused them
    to retreat:
*Chorus:*
Then fight and don't surrender but come when duty calls,
With heart and hand and sword and shield, we'll guard Old
    Derry's Walls.

That is just one part of the story, one view of history, and again if we look round other different parts of Belfast and the other towns and villages we find a very different interpretation. Each understanding of history is locked into the other and one is the counterpoint of the other. Here in West Belfast and elsewhere the wall drawings recall the great events of resistance to English rule in Ireland. The signal dates are 1641 – the Rebellion of the Irish against the Planters; 1798 – The United Irish Rebellion; 1916 – The Easter Rising and 1980 – The Hunger Strike and those who died in it. The portraits of the patriots such as Wolfe Tone, Padraic Pearse and James Connolly and others who were executed after the Easter Rising in Dublin in 1916 are featured.

Corrymeela has helped me to understand how a vast number of young adults think as they grow up in this divided society. What a confusing environment in which to live! There are so many opposing signs and uncertain leads. They have known from birth where it is safe to go and the areas to be avoided. They cannot miss the multitudes of slogans and murals that cover the gable ends and walls where they live. These confront them with two violently opposed ways of life and use cultural, historic, political and religious symbols to get their message across. One I remember very specially from the Hunger Strike period was a pietà, the prone body of Christ resting in his mother's arms and below the words:

Blessed are those who hunger and thirst for justice.

Again the division of the churches and the separate-school system compound their confusion. Even social and sporting activities are different. One side plays hurley and Gaelic football, while the other concentrates on football, hockey and cricket.

The tragic irony is that the one common problem that each side has to deal with, is lack of work. In some parts of the country there is 30–40 per cent unemployment. It is difficult for those who have never been without work to understand the sense of worthlessness and boredom that is felt. So there is one graffito that applies right across the barriers. It reads simply:

Is there life before death?

But there is a change taking place. Many of those who come to Corrymeela are very critical of the old prejudices and attitudes. Pop culture has a deep influence, but there is more to it than that. I have noticed this change in radio and TV discussions featuring teenagers at school. A great number now are ready for cross-community experiences and that is why Corrymeela has been committed from the start to a wide range of experimental programmes for young people.

Probably the most deep-seated area of conflict is the economic one. Ireland has always been on the edge of British and European economy and has suffered from constant lack of employment. It is here that young people are most affected. This has been the centre of intense competition for the jobs that are available. The facts show that young Catholics usually come off second best. There has been much evidence of discrimination against Catholics and this has left a smouldering sense of injustice. It is not by chance that most of the violence originates in the areas of economic deprivation. This is a most sensitive issue, as the efforts of the Fair Employment Agency indicate. The words of Lord Brookeborough who was Prime Minister from 1943–65 are still remembered and frequently quoted, when he declared proudly in public that he would not have a Catholic in his employ, and that Catholics were 'out to destroy Ulster with all their might and power'. This illustrates the depth of fear that existed then and still exists and with it the sense of insecurity that lies deep in the Protestant psyche.

Here then we have the anatomy of the Northern Irish conflict. Commentators, political analysts, and historians endlessly debate priorities. Is it basically cultural, political, religious, or economic? All I would say is that each of them has to be faced.

For me I prefer to emphasize the harsh realities that lie behind all the analysis and debate; the depth of hate, fear and uncertainty which many in Belfast face each day. I could include other areas outside the city, but I stay with Belfast, because I know it best.

One of the most chastening experiences for me comes when I have to accompany a group of visitors from other countries who have come to Corrymeela to learn about Ireland. The idea is to let them see not the tourist attractions and the beautiful parks and listed buildings, but rather the other face of the city.

So our minibus slowly makes its way around the areas of chronic unemployment, narrow streets, much derelict housing – though redevelopment work is making considerable progress. Still there are many signs of urban decay with vandalized multi-storey blocks and desolate waste spaces. As we move around we are conscious of the strong security presence, the checkpoints, the no-parking areas, the large gates that can seal off a street if trouble erupts. From time to time military vehicles pass with helmeted soldiers peering out with their weapons at the ready and sometimes their faces obscured by their plastic visors. Frequently the strident klaxon of a police car followed by an ambulance announces another bomb alert to be checked. Occasionally a loud explosion is heard and we wonder how near we are to the place. Often the atmosphere is filled with the persistent and noisy chopping of an army helicopter hovering above some potential trouble spot. All these serve to create an atmosphere of tenseness and anxiety. Finally our visitors see just how real the polarization is, as we stop at a high solid brick wall down the side of a street. This marks the 'Peace Line' that divides part of West Belfast. It reminds me of the Berlin Wall I had seen years ago.

I begin to think of some of those I know in this area. I first met Maureen three years ago, when a relative who had worked at Corrymeela asked me to call and see her. She lives with her two young sons in a short street in North Belfast. I called to express my sympathy at the death of her husband Sean. He had been shot in their home by a Protestant paramilitary group, and it had been another case of mistaken identity. I had attended the funeral and in some small way been able to share in the pain and hurt and anger of the relatives. The funeral service was very dignified and the homily of the priest most moving.

Maureen is a brave person, and articulate. There was no self-pity but a deep concern for the way this was affecting her children. She showed me photographs of their wedding. They were a very happy and united family. Her irreplaceable loss and sorrow is only one of thousands of other homes that have suffered in a similar way because a solution has not be found for the conflict.

I call in at a different place. It is not a home but a fruit market close to where we live. I go there usually to buy fruit. This time I went there to sympathize with the staff. A few days before two IRA terrorists had driven into the market, stopped their car, as if to collect some fruit. They went over to the owner's office and pulled a gun and shot him. When I arrived there, the staff were still in a state of shock. They showed me the spot where their boss had been shot. I could see the place had been recently washed, but the bullet marks were still there. He had been a fair man and liked by his staff.

What was the reason for the shooting? The IRA said it would shoot anyone who supplied goods to the army. I understood that the firm had never been asked whether they did or did not. He was a young man in his early forties with several children in his family.

This is just another illustration of what thousands of families have had to face in this tiny country of one-and-a-half million and about the size of Yorkshire, over the last twenty years.

Here then is the core of the conflict – the political, religious, social and cultural realities and some of the results in the pain and suffering, the hate and the destruction that continue because the conflict has not been solved.

I know that I cannot detach myself from it. This is my

problem. These are my people. I must be involved though at times I would love to opt out. I am also part of the conflict. My Davey forebears were part of the Plantation. Miskimmon's History of Carrickfergus tells me that the Daveys came there in the sixteenth century. They are among the few families mentioned. There is still a Davy Street in the town. One family tree suggests family links back to Robert the Bruce. It is also claimed that one member of the family achieved the distinction of being hanged, adding, at a safe distance, a peculiar lustre to the family tree.

And yet, as I am aware of my roots, I have also become conscious of the other tradition. Through the privilege of many friends I have been able to listen to and understand their story, and in a real way share their hurts and fears, as they have mine. I have come to see how close we are and that we all love this land. Underneath there is the strong desire among an increasing number that we live together appreciating and respecting each other's way of life and culture. I can see the challenge to carry through these hopes and the role we have to play together in such communities as Corrymeela with many others. I believe the politics of violence and confrontation can change into co-operation and trust. Sooner or later a new order will begin to emerge, in which the dignity and worth of each person will be recognized and the integrity of each tradition cherished.

This hope comes through to me as I see the changes that are taking place here and there in our country. The signs are increasing throughout the land that all sorts of people – school children, students, ordinary citizens, trades unions, workers, churchpeople, peace groups and community groups are restless for a better and peaceful society. At the same time, in case we be accused of unrealistic euphoria and wishful thinking, we know the difficulties and setbacks that lie ahead. Day by day we are grimly reminded of those who believe that the only way to bring about change is by the trigger of a gun or the fuse of a time bomb.

The good Lord gives each of us from time to time those little hints, signs that He is about, if we have the eyes to see them. This is such a one that was given to Kathleen and myself along with Father Tony Farquhar, who was at that time one of the Catholic chaplains at Queen's University. He is now Auxiliary Bishop in the Diocese of Down and Connor. The three of us had travelled to Lausanne in Switzerland to tell about the work of Corrymeela. It was the Week of Prayer for Christian Unity and we had a very full programme of meetings, services and interviews.

One afternoon we had a pause in our itinerary and our gracious hosts decided that we needed a break, so they drove us away up into the snow-capped mountains and through a quiet peaceful landscape, until we came to a little village called Romain Moitier. When we got out of the car they led us to a beautiful Romanesque church which they thought would interest us. No sooner had we entered the foyer than we began to understand why they had brought us to this place. On the wall immediately facing us as we entered there was a large map of ancient Europe. Ireland on the edge of it was marked out with a red circle.

Across Holland, Belgium, France, Germany and Switzerland certain places were underlined. As we studied it we could see that it was the story of the Irish missionaries of the Celtic period in the fifth to ninth centuries who had journeyed from their different houses in Ireland. We can think of Columbanus who came from the monastery in Bangor, County Down, and had established Christian Communities in many parts of Europe. One of his followers, St Gall, made a profound and lasting impression in Switzerland. You may guess how moved we were to learn that this Christian House in Romain Moitier had been founded by Irish missionaries. Then Ireland was described as 'the land of saints and scholars' and the Irish known as the great missionary race.

In the silence we thought about it and above all the sadness of our visit. Here we were many centuries later, representing the

Catholic and Protestant traditions in Ireland, coming to this country to try to explain the division and tragedy of our land, the same Ireland, centuries later. Before we left the church, we stood together with joined hands in the Sanctuary, and after saying the Lord's Prayer we prayed that through the healing of the Spirit our land might again become 'the land of saints and scholars'.

# CHAPTER NINE

# *Community*

*For he has made known to us . . . the mystery of his will . . . to unite all things in Christ, things in heaven and things on earth.*
EPHESIANS 1:9--10

*What life have you, if you have not life together?*
*There is no life that is not in community,*
*And no community not lived in praise of God.* T.S. ELIOT

For a long time we have kept a small globe of the world in our front bay window. It is to remind us and our friends that we are all part of the one world human family.

In every one of us there is that inner yearning to belong, to participate, to be in relationship and in community. That is how we are made and what it means to be human. That is just how I felt when with millions of others all round the world I watched the Barcelona Olympic Games in July '92. That seemingly unending procession of nations round the huge arena, all so different and yet so united and happy to be together, and so much at one with the vast crowd of spectators seen and unseen and so thrilled to celebrate the joy of their common humanity.

Every day our ecologists, our economists and politicians warn us that this togetherness is not a romantic idea to be celebrated every four years, but a vital necessity. It is a matter of community or chaos. We now live in the one global village and will survive or perish together. But isn't this what the Bible is all about – that God has made us to be one family and find our unity in Him? That is the Good News.

But there is, alas, the Bad News. The other grim reality – the urge we have to reject community. We want 'to do our own thing' and have our own way. So the terrible trinity of jealousy, pride and rivalry break up and destroy our peace, and our own 'god-almightiness' takes over. The Greek word for devil is *diabolos,* the one who breaks up, divides and tears apart. So we have 'ethnic cleansing', Hitler's 'final solution', and our self-interested sectarianism with all its lethal results.

But there is the Good News again. God does not give us up or throw in His hand. In spite of everything He continues to call us to join in His great dancing circle of celebration and hope:

> Where the morning stars shone together
> And all the sons of God shouted for joy.

Although some refuse to join the circle and others turn aside to form their own, the Dance goes on for He is Lord of the Dance.

> 'I danced on the Friday when the sky turned black.
> It's hard to dance with the devil on your back.
> They buried my body and they thought I'd gone,
> But I am the Dance and I still go on.
>
> They cut me down and I leapt up high.
> I am the life that'll never never die.
> I'll live in you if you live in me.
> I am the Lord of the Dance', said he.

'But how', you ask, 'do you work this out at Corrymeela?' The best answer I can give is to take you on a visit to the place itself. So we drive from Belfast, some sixty miles up County Antrim along an excellent motorway and dual carriage road, and in slightly over an hour I am able to point out the lovely Moyle Bay, setting off the massive splendour of Fair Head, and far beyond, the dim outline of the Mull of Kintyre. Then slowly we drop down into the pleasant and historic town of Ballycastle. We pass through the Diamond where each August the 400-year-old Lammas Fair is held. A straight road leads us down to the seafront. We turn right and cross the Margy Bridge. On our right the ruins of Bonamargy, a fourteenth-century Franciscan Priory, remind us that our Christian Community is no new idea, but that we are indeed part of the one, holy, catholic and apostolic church, transcending time and space. I am sure those who have once lived and prayed there and are now in the fuller life, look down on us and our efforts with joy, and as we pass by, bless us in the words of their prayer:

> May the road rise with you,
> May the wind be always on your back:
> May the sun shine warm on your face
> And may the Lord hold you in the hollow of his hand.

The road bisects the golf course as we come right on to the coastline. The vibrant fresh air with the tumbling breakers lift our spirits. Our way forks right, as we speed up a steep hill. A long turn brings the white outline of Corrymeela into sight against the distant background of Knocklayd – the Broad Hill – and we have arrived. This approach is in itself a very potent part of the Corrymeela experience. A great number of those who come are from the drabness of the inner city or the monotony of a housing estate. As one little girl who had just arrived said: 'Corrymeela is a great place – the Park is at the door'. Or there was the little boy who said as he left: 'Goodbye sea, goodbye sky, goodbye Heaven'. It has healing and peace and hope. You can understand why one of the constant themes of the daily worship is just 'the celebration of creation'. Another Celtic prayer is often on our lips:

> Deep peace of the running wave to you
> Deep peace of the flowing wind to you
> Deep peace of the quiet earth to you
> Deep peace of the shining stars to you
> Deep peace of the Son of peace to you.

Kathleen Bakewell greets us very warmly at reception. Largely through her we have come to realize just how important this is. Many who come for the first time are very shy and unsure of what Corrymeela is about. Often, through their own experiences, they feel very vulnerable. One such lady came with her family and later commented: 'As soon as I entered the door I knew that I was welcome and wanted.' Kathleen though will tell you of the occasional hiccups that do arise:

> There is always the problem of communication. Recently an Irish priest rang from London to say that he and several others were on a pilgrimage to Knock and wondered if they could visit Corrymeela en route to County Mayo. I replied that we would be delighted to receive them and provide a meal. You may guess my utter dismay when two huge buses arrived packed with some 100 pilgrims. An emergency group was immediately recruited to make sandwiches and the Burco boiler brought out of storage. The mottos is: Always beware of Irish understatement.

As Corrymeela is a dispersed community, the times we have together are very special, especially the residential periods at Ballycastle. A large number of the 160-plus membership come from all parts of Northern Ireland, a few from the Republic and others also make the journey from England and Scotland. It is a time when we can catch up with each other's news and share our lives. It gives us all an opportunity to learn what is happening in the different parts of the programme, and also to discuss and at times debate issues that have arisen and initiatives that our Community should take.

Our membership is for the most part lay people with a small sprinkling of clergy – (if that is an appropriate description!) They represent different strata of society and include people from conservative and radical backgrounds. Some are close relatives of people who have been killed in the violence, while others are former prisoners. You will meet single parents and some unemployed. There are school and university teachers. Quite a few are social workers, and the older professions too are represented, including the civil service, the church, industry, agriculture and commerce. Nor must we forget those active in local and national politics.

We are all bound together by our commitment to Christian reconciliation. That is the common ground on which we meet. But we are very conscious that reconciliation applies not only to communal violence, but to many other areas as well. We know that reconciliation, like peace, is indivisible. So in our living as a community and in our programme we try to face other areas of conflict such as the generation gap, sexual equality, exploitation of resources, poverty and unemployment. In our situation the greatest division is between Catholic and Protestant. From the start much of our energy has been used in breaking this historic barrier. People living outside Ireland do not realize how deep-seated it is. Both words are weighed down by great burdens of political and cultural baggage. This has meant that the realities of each Christian tradition are almost blotted out by mythology, misinformation and exploitation. This situation is greatly compounded by the very limited opportunities large sections of the population have to meet and get to know each other.

This was brought home to me by what Cathie, a fifteen-year-old Catholic girl from West Belfast, said to me: 'Corrymeela is a lovely place – because there is no religion here.' I knew that she regularly took part in morning and evening worship. But that, to her, was not what religion was about. For her it meant hatred, fear and violence. This is a most cruel theft of language.

Somehow an atmosphere of openness, of trust, and of acceptance has been given to us at Corrymeela. It is a gift. It could not have been planned by any committee or inspired by any resolution. I know it is God's gift given through the varied membership at different stages in their spiritual journey, who have been drawn together because they hunger and thirst for a just and peaceful country, the Kingdom of God in Ireland. So it has the mark of a genuine Christian Community, as the members are largely 'task-orientated rather than self-orientated', to use John Harvey of Iona's phrase. It is through the dedication and devotion of a great number of people that Corrymeela continues. Some are very articulate in their belief and at home in religious and church language. Some others find this difficult but show by what they do how deep their concern is for the practical operation of Corrymeela. I think of those who give limitlessly of their time in driving the buses, installing and maintaining the electrical system, tending the garden and mowing the grass, in carpentry, painting and plumbing. Then there are those who will look after small children to give their parents a break, nor can I omit those who cook, clean and administrate. Some of them would find it difficult to talk about religion, or lead in prayer, but they pray in the way they live, and without verbalizing it, make the fruits of the Spirit visible: love, joy, peace, patience, kindness, fidelity, humility and self-control.

As time passes I become more and more aware of that great crowd of people all over these islands and far beyond, on the Continent, in America, Australia and New Zealand who keep Corrymeela in their prayers.

I once spoke in a very small town in Australia, quite a long train journey from Melbourne, and deep in the country. I told them of what Corrymeela was trying to do. At the end an elderly lady who had long since emigrated from Ireland came up to speak to me. She simply said: 'I'll never see you again, but I want you to know that I'll be praying for Corrymeela.' Then she embraced me.

This world-wide support brings home to us the reality of Christian solidarity, as does the remarkable and moving letter Canon Horace Dammers of Coventry Cathedral received from a Benedictine abbey in Peru. He had sent an appeal for Corrymeela's work of Christian Reconciliation. In the letter of reply the monks thanked him for the appeal and promised to

*ove:* A warm welcome awaits all visitors to Corrymeela

mmerfest attracts a great number of visitors every third year

The Croi (Gaelic for the heart), the central place for meeting, worship and celebration

The Tree of Life is a collage mounted on a three-part sliding screen. It was designed and made by Lisa Andrews of Eton as a perpetual reminder of our unity in our diversity

*Above:* All-age worship in the Croi

Work-camps have always been an important part of Corrymeela

A group of one-year volunteers who come to Corrymeela from all over the world to serve and learn

Mother Teresa of Calcutta speaking at Summerfest in 1981

Children are especially welcome at Corrymeela

A carefree holiday

A wartime photo
sent home to
Kathleen from a
Dresden prison
camp, August 1944

A recent photo of Kathleen and Ray

Our enviable clifftop location!

Sunset at Corryme[...]

What we are
all about!

CORRYMEELA
*IS*
PEOPLE OF ALL AGES
AND CHRISTIAN TRADITIONS,
WHO, INDIVIDUALLY AND
TOGETHER ARE COMMITTED
TO THE HEALING OF SOCIAL,
RELIGIOUS & POLITICAL DIVISIONS
THAT EXIST IN NORTHERN IRELAND,
AND THROUGHOUT
THE WORLD

pray for Corrymeela. Then the letter went on to describe their own situation in Peru. Their abbey had been destroyed in an earthquake and some of the monks killed. Now they were just beginning to recover. Their letter ended:

> It has taken all we had to do these small works. We feel very much as St Peter. Silver, gold, there's none that I have, but in Christ Jesus' name a blessing upon your good works.

But what is the heart of Corrymeela? What is its spirituality?

Some time ago I wrote a leaflet about Corrymeela and entitled it: 'The place where you don't need to whisper'. That is part of the intangible dynamic that has been given to us. I can only speak personally about this. For me it has been a time of continual learning about other people, about community and about myself. At the start I had many simplistic and romantic ideas. It would just work out as we met together, I thought. But it wasn't like that. Good relationships don't come easily or cheaply and it is painful to learn about one's own limitations and prejudices. Add to this the difficulty of accepting those whose ideas and opinions and, at times, personalities clash, and the importance of openness before God and before each other becomes essential. Only in an atmosphere of trust can we accept people as they are, and find ourselves accepted too.

So acceptance, sharing and listening have become more and more important for us. This brings us near to the heart of community life. It has become a place where people can relax, be free to be themselves and open to others. Here images, status and the various masks we use, are discarded. You know what happens when you have a real talk with another person. Very often a new relationship is born. In the sharing of our stories a meeting of minds and spirits takes place and trust is established.

I believe that this is the way the Spirit works, though often we are unaware of what is happening. John Taylor uses a revealing phrase to describe the way the Holy Spirit works. He is: 'The Go-

Between God'. To me that is a meaningful description. 'God the Spirit' says Taylor 'is the unceasing animator and communicator, the inexhaustible source of insight, awareness, recognition and response.' The reality of this comes home to me more and more at Corrymeela.

One of our members speaks for us all when she said that for her 'Corrymeela is a Christian way, following Christ, looking to the gospels, a Christian community, living in relationship with others, which gives me a place, allows me to be, and helps me to endure the darkness and to light a candle no matter how small.'

It is specially meaningful when it takes place across the catastrophic divisions of politics, tradition, class, generation and sex. Tommy O'Rourke was a pensioner from the Protestant Shankill Road. He came with a group for a week's break at Corrymeela. Sister Vincentia, a nun from the Cross and Passion Convent in Ballycastle came up regularly to help with these groups of senior citizens. In the course of the week Tommy struck up quite a friendship with the sister. Towards the end of the time someone said to him: 'Tommy, ye're gettin' on very well with that wee nun.' 'She's not a nun,' was his indignant reply, 'she's the District Nurse.' But something very important had happened to Tommy. He had had a real meeting, a relationship had developed. The stereotype had been broken and his idea of a nun completely transformed. He had encountered the real person and had not even noticed that she was a nun, much less a member of the 'other side'.

The core team at Ballycastle is led by Colin Craig, the Centre Director in partnership with Rachel, his talented wife. Colin first came as a schoolboy and then after university and subsequently becoming Project Director of the National Children's Homes for North West England, came back to Corrymeela. He is an expert canoeist and has led expeditions round Cape Horn and to other hazardous locations. These skills of leadership and 'navigation' are most important in a place like Corrymeela. The core group is twenty-nine strong, some living in and others living in the

Ballycastle area. With such a demanding programme of some 250–300 groups coming each year, countless visitors and many unpredictable people and events to deal with, it is a most demanding task for each of them. I sometimes marvel at their patience and good humour. I was very moved by what Brenda Stewart, the leader of the housekeeping staff, once replied when asked about her work: 'To me Corrymeela is a unique place. Everyone is accepted here, and made to feel they matter and have something to give.'

Yet it is important to be honest and realistic about the ongoing life of Corrymeela. Sometimes we have visitors who come with the most romantic and idealistic ideas about the Centre and the people. I would emphasize that they have never lived there! It would be strange if in such a mixed group of people there were not at times tensions and disagreements. Corrymeela is, after all, just a group of ordinary normal human beings. We are part of a divided society and we do share these divisions. This is what John Morrow has said: 'It is essential that we always recognize that the conflicts that exist in our society . . . are present in a degree among us. As a community we are only beginning to understand each other.'

Frequently I have travelled abroad, to the United States, to the Continent and Australia, to tell the story of our Community. When I return, climb up the hill and see Corrymeela once again, I pause and ask myself: 'Is this *really* the place you have been talking about?'

Easter Day 1991 marked the 25th year of our Community. We wanted to celebrate this by doing something very special. Our problem was how could we do justice to all that Corrymeela had meant to us, the people we had met, many from afar, the events that had taken place and how much it had changed our lives. Above all, we wanted to give thanks to God for his guiding Spirit through the years, leading us on and holding us all together. We thought of different things – a service or a concert or the visit of some VIP. Then the idea came – a pilgrimage around the grounds of Corrymeela, marking the different places of significance on our journey. This idea was immediately accepted.

Everyone, members, friends and children – all could participate. We knew it was specially appropriate, as we were all on an unfinished journey. We had passed through many hazards and excitements. Now we needed to take stock together and prepare for what lay ahead. So two hundred of us made our way round the six stations that we had planned.

We set out from 'the Cottages', the site of the first work camps. In our songs, prayers and readings we remembered those who had done the pioneering work. Many of us thought that Billy McAllister, the first and much loved warden of 1965, was not far away:

> And you will speed us onward with a cheer
> And wave beyond the stars that all is well

We moved on, led by the volunteers and Colin Craig. They carried long standards, bearing thin yellow pennants that flapped and fluttered in the wind. The chants of Taizé and Iona quickened us on our way.

'The Village' has always been the focal point of the many youth programmes that have been carried out through the years, and we stopped there to give thanks for the dedicated work of many youth leaders through the years. I associate this part of our programme especially with Billy Kane who was the first full-time youth co-ordinator. I had the chance of working with him from time to time. Billy developed many different models in his approach to young adults, most of whom were unemployed and came from areas where there was frequent violence. He had a great gift in getting close to them, identifying with them and understanding their needs. On one occasion he took a group to Dublin to watch an international football match. Most of the party had seldom, if ever, been out of Belfast, let alone cross the Border. The match was between Northern Ireland and the Republic of Ireland. Billy's group was mixed – Roman Catholic and Protestant. Both had problems with flags and emblems. The Catholics were supporting Northern Ireland but found it impossible to sport the Union Jack. Nor could they wave the Tricolour, as that would have been for the wrong side. The same problem faced the young Protestants when their team was playing England. They solved their difficulty by inventing a green and white flag. These experiences started off a very vigorous debate among them, as to who they really were, the nature of their identity and indeed the whole question of the conflict which was so much part of their lives.

But many other very different groups have stayed in the Village. Yvonne Naylor, a teacher in a school for severely handicapped children, tells this story:

> Once, when we were staying at Corrymeela with our children from the school, we called in at the House to meet the people who were staying there. They were senior citizens with all the usual problems of failing vision and hearing, arthritis and restricted mobility. They were a bit shy of our children at first, all of them physically handicapped, many in wheelchairs, three profoundly deaf and signing to each other. Our children made themselves at home, went up to some of the old people smiling and gesturing, one of them throwing open her arms to greet an old lady who was just delighted. Everyone was 'at home', mutually encouraging one another. I heard one lady say to another, 'Aren't those children an inspiration? I won't complain about my arthritis for at least a month!' And although on arrival they had complained about not being able to get about very much, they regularly came over to the Village to join in the fun, exchanging gifts of love and joy.

Our pilgrimage moves us on to the next station – Coventry House. Here we give thanks for the incredible support

Corrymeela has had through the years from so many countries.

Coventry House itself was largely funded by the Cross of Nails Network, operating from Coventry Cathedral. The London Corrymeela Link who took up the challenge from Coventry then raised most of the money to provide the Croi – the worship and meeting place for all the different groups on site together. More recently the baton has been passed on to the Corrymeela Link, based in Reading, who have continued their support over fifteen years. Nor can the backing from America, Australia, Germany, Switzerland and Holland be forgotten.

Many of these countries have not stopped there, but have encouraged and financed young people to come and work alongside us. This to me is personalized by Doug Baker, an American Presbyterian Minister who came to us some years ago. Doug fell in love with Ireland and later with his Irish wife, Elaine. He has made an immense contribution in the field of Christian education, the most significant being the five day 'Summerfest' every third year at the beginning of July. This is a time when Corrymeela really goes public. Several hundred live at Corrymeela and others in local hotels and boarding houses. Also a large number of people come with their families for a day. The programme is designed to include every member of the family. There are children and young adult programmes, workshops, sharing groups, concerts and plenary sessions with world-renowned Christian leaders. Who but Doug could have persuaded Mother Teresa, Beyers Naude, Sheila Cassidy, Elias Chacour, Hans Ruedi Weber, Pauline Webb, Jean Vanier, in addition to 'the Liverpool Twins', Derek Worlock and David Sheppard, to come and speak at Summerfest? Summerfest makes us not only aware of our own problems but also the needs and challenges of the wider world.

Our mood changes as we move to the Memorial Playground, our fourth station. Here we are suddenly reminded of the terrible cost of these years of violence and killing, and the pain and sorrow so many in Corrymeela, and in the wider community, continue to endure. This playground was opened in May 1986 in memory of Sean Armstrong, the thirty-one-year-old field officer of the International Voluntary Trust, who was shot at the entrance to his flat in South Belfast. He had been threatened by extremists from both sides, because of his efforts to bring children of all traditions together, but refused to give up his work. I knew him well and had often co-operated with him in different projects. In addition his parents were very old friends of mine.

Sean's assassination, in a very special way, represents the awesome tragedy and futility of the conflict. He was a most attractive and gifted person, representing what was best and most creative in our society. He inspired the establishment of the Glebe House, a mini Corrymeela, in Strangford, County Down, and had given all his talents and energy to underprivileged children, in organizing cross-community work camps, holidays and exchange programmes.

This children's playground reminds us of the price so many have had to pay, and Sean's life and example will always remain to inspire and challenge us, as we pass by.

The mood changes again as we move on to the front lawn overlooking the sea – Station 5. This is a place of hope, a place where we look out beyond Ireland and into the future. It is a place of vision and new possibilities. Very appropriately the young adults took over. It was Easter Day – they called us all to join hands in a great circle, as we sang 'Lord of the Dance'. Here we proclaimed the Easter message of the Risen Christ. He is Lord of all and his victory over evil, hate, fear and death itself has begun and will be completed. We ended with the great affirmation:

> In the midst of hatred and death
> We celebrate the promise of love and life
> In the midst of sin and decay
> We celebrate the promise of salvation and renewal
> In the midst of the dying Lord
> We celebrate the promise of the living Christ.

Finally we, like everyone who visits Corrymeela, arrive at the Croi (the Heart). For us-all it is a very special place and brings together both the roots and elements of Christian Community in a living experience. Norman Hawthorne, the architect, told us that when he planned it he had shades of Skellig Michael, off Dingle in County Kerry, in his mind. It was an early Christian settlement, built on the very fringe of Europe during the fifth and sixth centuries, when Christianity was driven out from the Eastern Mediterranean. Once again we are reminded of the depth of our roots and that great succession of those gone before us.

Sometimes I like to sit in the quiet of the Croi and remember all those who come here through the year to pray: the politicians, the teachers, the social workers, community leaders, many with their young people; the different clergy and theologians; those in the arts; and multitudes of others concerned to face together the cultural, political and religious differences. In addition the many young people, hurt and trapped by the unemployment and violence they have known all their lives. There are those whose menfolk are in jail and also many who have lost a loved one in the violence. Here the divide is crossed, as Catholics and Protestants pray together.

The Croi is an open place. It is not for any particular group or tradition but for all. It is for those who try to follow Christ and those who have not reached that stage, but want to be here.

It is a place of reflection and challenge, where Bonhöffer's question is often asked: 'What does it mean to follow Christ today?'

It is a place of celebration and hope. There are times of laughter and joy with songs and music and drama. Sometimes it is a place of sadness and tears, where the bereaved and broken find hope and strength.

The most adequate description is in this poem, written and spoken at the service of Dedication in July 1979 by Canon Reggie Askew, the pioneer of the London Venture Group, who raised the funds to make the Croi possible:

The Croi is like an ear,
A great intricate ear to catch prayers in.
It is a trumpet wound round
Into a winding horn for sounding praise,
for heralding good news.
What a singing place this is
When you open your mouth!
How you improve your voice!

But it is also a nice place
For hide and seek, a secret dwelling,
A stronghold inviting mystery.
The first Christians were on the run:
They dodged into catacombs like this.
It is a quiet place
For the bones of saints to lie in,
A good Irish king would wish
To be buried here.

Simple and white as Easter
It describes the tomb of Christ,
From whence our resurrection springs.
The place is set for Easter morning.
It has the dimensions of an egg,
The possibilities of new life.

And I know that people will come
At once and use it in different ways.
Children will see plainly it is
Obviously a space ship padded in the earth,
Primed for patrolling the stars,
With round hatches rolling about.
And hermits will regard it as a cyclotron,
A machine for accelerating prayer.
And dancing folk will join hands
And make a ring without thinking.

And those who like feasting
Will make a table round
And sit like kings, in order
To welcome Christ's supper here
Above the sea shore.

But we must remember that Ballycastle is only part of Corrymeela. Otherwise it could easily be thought of as a pleasant place of escape, where those who come can 'get away from it all'. It is indeed the shop window, the place that people know about. But it is part of a much wider network. Corrymeela House in Belfast shares with Ballycastle as the twin axis on which the community operates. Each is complementary to the other.

The importance of this relationship came home to me graphically in the following incident. A group of English and Scottish friends and supporters came over to Corrymeela for a weekend. They wanted to learn about the Irish problem and the Community's programme of reconciliation. On the Sunday afternoon they left Ballycastle and came to Belfast for the final session. As an introduction to their discussion, they were taken in the Corrymeela bus round some of the trouble spots in west Belfast. Billy Kane and John Morrow were doing the commentary. All went well until they were passing from the Protestant Shankill to the Catholic Ardoyne. Suddenly they landed right into a street fight between rival factions. It was too late to turn back. Immediately the stones and petrol bombs stopped. The Corrymeela bus was recognized by both sides and allowed to continue on its way in safety. Once they were past, the fight continued. At the final session in Corrymeela House, this last experience dominated the discussion, as the visitors now understood in a very real way what Corrymeela at Ballycastle and elsewhere was all about.

Corrymeela House is the communication centre for the life and work of the community. It is the main base for the leader, the bursar, administrative staff, as well as the five field workers.

Here most of the key committees and planning groups meet.

The House is also shared with many other groups who work in co-operation with us in the wider society. Examples are the Mixed Marriage Association, Work Party on Faith and Politics, Amnesty International, Current Affairs, Cross-Community Youth Groups, Follow-up programmes and prayer cells.

The House can be a marketplace where all the world is coming and going; buses arriving from Ballycastle or leaving for it; groups waiting to be collected or arriving for a Belfast-orientated programme; young unemployed people dropping in for a chat; people calling in to find out about our programmes; teachers, social workers, clergy etc. seeking out staff, enquiring about bookings, or just looking for someone to listen to their problems. In the midst of this the phones do not cease to ring with calls from near and far. A family is being intimidated, can we help with temporary accommodation? A group from Women's Aid wants to book a room; somebody forgot their luggage – was it sent on? Some item for the Corrymeela Fair is delivered; paint arrives to be taken to Ballycastle; the *Corrymeela News* is ready to be collected and so it goes on.

Most members can only travel to Ballycastle occasionally. After all we are a dispersed community, but contact and keeping in touch with each other and Corrymeela is vital, if we are to be a living community. So scattered through the country there are eighteen cells or house groups. There are similar meetings in different parts of England and Scotland. Usually the host or hostess for the evening reads a short act of worship. Perhaps a speaker is invited or a suitable book used for study or occasionally a video. Most groups have projects, sometimes at Corrymeela such as running a family week for underprivileged people, or planning a stall at the Corrymeela Fair. The great value of such small meetings is that those who come have time to get to know each other, to support and encourage those going through times of stress, and also to do things together in their own area.

The Community's direction is in the hands of a council,

elected by the members at the AGM. The leader has the task of implementing the decisions of council. Also he is expected to provide leadership to the whole Community, its members and staff. He is also there to remind members of the vision of Corrymeela and its spiritual foundations. In addition he spends much time in communicating the Corrymeela message to the wider society of Northern Ireland and further afield.

John Morrow, as leader over the past thirteen years, has had the massive task of keeping the Community on course, and at the same time holding it together in all its diversity. Recently I heard a recording of a programme about Eric Ashby, when he was Vice Chancellor of Queen's University. He was asked to explain his role as head of the university. He described how he saw himself resembling the five-pound weight that was placed on top of the saucepan lid as the Christmas pudding is cooked. Its task was to hold down the rich and bubbling mixture below. That is also an excellent description of the Corrymeela leader's task. I think of all the ingredients that make up the Corrymeela Community: the diversity of membership in age, background, interests and concerns. Then there are those times of tension and debate, when hard decisions have to be made. There is also the constant support and listening to those facing difficult personal problems or decisions.

John has held down this complex and lively mixture, not by the weight of authoritarianism or guile, but by his clarity of mind, his integrity and humility, his humanity and compassion, and a very quick sense of humour. In all John's work through the years Shirley has been a magnificent partner. In her own right she has made a most significant contribution to the on-going life of the Community, acting on several committees, involved in women and family programmes in addition to constant hospitality in their home in Belfast. It is said that when St Columba upbraided one of his disciples on Iona, the sound of his voice could be heard across in Mull. I don't know if John Morrow's voice would carry as far as our Rathlin Island, but I do believe that when there is an off-shore breeze blowing from

Corrymeela, the sound of his laughter can be heard across the Waters of Moyle.

# CHAPTER TEN

# Peacemaking

*Blessed are the peacemakers.* MATTHEW 5:9

*For Christ is our peace, who has made us both one, and has broken down the dividing wall of hostility.* EPHESIANS 2:14

The Corrymeela Community is a response to those words of Jesus. In the service of dedication at the beginning of each year members make this commitment:

> We surrender ourselves to the Spirit of Jesus to overcome our divisions and make us instruments of His peace.

On Saturday 14th August 1976 Kathleen and I set out for Finaghy, a suburb of Belfast. It was a warm sunny afternoon, but nobody was concerned about the weather. As we turned off the Lisburn Road and approached the railway bridge in Finaghy Road North, we joined in with more and more people who were on the same journey. They were mostly silent and grim faced as they walked along. Four days earlier there had been a car chase involving the IRA and the army. The driver of the escaping vehicle was hit and his vehicle, out of control, lurched across the footway and crashed into the perimeter fence of the Saint John the Baptist Primary School. Two young children were killed instantly and a third mortally injured. They were all children of Anne Maguire, who was herself badly injured.

Mairead Corrigan, Anne's sister and aunt of the children, was so stunned and appalled at what had happened that she decided something had to be done. She was joined by Betty Williams and Ciaran McKeown and the Peace Movement was launched. This massive response showed how multitudes of people felt. The road was crowded with 10,000 people. We were too far away to hear what was said, but the sense of outrage and disgust was palpable and words were not needed. Just to be there where it had happened and be together with so many people was an unforgettable experience. Close by on the roof of a garage a few IRA supporters jeered at the crowd. They were obviously alarmed at the turn of events. Massive support followed. The Peace People, as they came to be called, held marches all over Ireland and across the Irish Sea in Liverpool and Trafalgar Square. Later the two women were awarded the Nobel Peace Prize for 1976. But the tide was beginning to turn against them. The IRA opposition grew in ferocity as we discovered in the Peace March on the Falls Road, when the participants were attacked with stones and bottles and sixteen people were injured.

Eventually the support began to diminish. Many postmortems were held. The movement had begun on a widespread upsurge of emotion. The vast media coverage raised public expectation to an impossible pitch. It was not realistic for such a widely based group to work out acceptable aims and strategy in such a short time. It is important to record that the Peace People are still active, but with a much lower public profile and a more realistic agenda.

I believe that in peacemaking these public events such as marches, vigils and services are important. True there was much rhetoric, euphoria and naivety in the early days of the peace groups and many of us in Corrymeela were part of it, and did get carried away with optimism at times. But there is one supreme thing that happened at this stage – vast numbers of people were challenged to take up some form of peacemaking. Some did fall away but many have kept on in different peace initiatives and programmes. So motivation was and continues to be a very vital part of the process of peacemaking. But it must not stop there; it must lead on to two further stages: understanding or analysis and, finally, appropriate action. We learned by experience that we have to keep all three in mind.

So analysis began to take over. John White, the political scientist, described this little country as the best analysed in history. Corrymeela was inundated by a continuous flow of reporters, journalists, TV and radio crews, sociologists and researchers. I was rather shaken, during a period of extreme pressure at Corrymeela, when I was asked by a German sociologist if I had done a methodological study of the conflict! Some local peace workers complained of 'analysis paralysis', and they felt, at such times of intense interrogation, like specimens pinned down on a board to be examined and dissected.

The difficulty was, no one could give a clear explanation of the conflict. Was it political, religious, social, or cultural? Once several of us from Corrymeela were asked to meet with a high-powered delegation of political commentators and senators from Washington D.C. At one point in the discussion there was a pause and one of the party, fixing his eye on me, said: 'Mr Davey, can you tell us in a sentence exactly what the problem here is?' I took a deep breath and replied: 'Which of the 150 theories do you want to discuss?' I was not trying to be funny, but rather to emphasize the problem. The difficulty is that every answer raises a question. Someone said to Conor Cruise O'Brien, writer, politician and academic, that the problem had nothing to do with religion, in fact it was a red herring. To this he replied: 'Well, if it is a red herring, it is a whale of a herring!'

For my part, I believe the problem is a combination of both religion and politics, and the other issues merely serve to embitter and intensify the conflict. In everyday conversation religious and political terms are interchangeable. One tradition can be described as 'the Unionists' or 'the Protestants', equally the other as 'the Nationalists' or 'the Catholics'.

When one religious tradition identifies itself totally with a particular political party the results are tragic. In this way political leaders have frequently been able to hijack religion and exploit it for their own ends. So street slogans appear: 'For God and Ulster', that is Protestant Ulster, or 'Mary Mother of Ireland', that is Catholic Ireland.

Frequently the churches in Ireland get a bad press abroad and I am glad to set the record straight. True, there are many church members and some churches who do willingly identify themselves and their church with a particular political ideology. But I would make it abundantly clear that there are a great number of churches and members who repudiate this position, and very strongly affirm that Jesus Christ is Lord of all, and our loyalty to him and his Kingdom transcends any political ideology. John Dunlop, the present Moderator of the Presbyterian Church and a founder member of Corrymeela, has put it very clearly: 'The Church has the responsibility to ensure that the Lord Jesus Christ and his Gospel are not captured, exploited and used for political purposes.'

Another significant response from the churches, though not officially, has been the continuing statements of a group of churchmen on the current situation. Two of our members, John Morrow, the leader of Corrymeela, and David Stevens, secretary of the Irish Council of Churches, are part of an ecumenical working party set up in 1983 at the suggestion of an interchurch meeting in Greenhills Monastery near Drogheda. They became known as 'An Interchurch Group on Faith and Politics in the Northern Ireland Conflict'. While this does not claim to be an official organ of the churches, it is not only ecumenical, but includes representatives from both parts of Ireland.

I believe this is a most important process in helping lay people in the churches and outside to face the theological, social and political implications of a sectarian religion. The reports have been blunt and direct in stating the dangers of the betrayal of the Gospel in Ireland. It is a continuing task, and to date eight booklets have appeared since 1985 in an attempt to keep in touch with an ever-changing situation. Hate and enmity form the Barrier Reef on which each political initiative is shipwrecked. When they are at the conference table the foundation of any meeting of minds or agreement is flawed and insecure. They eclipse trust and confidence.

'Hatred and fear stem directly from idolatry and injustice.'

Both go together as the Old Testament makes clear. If you obey false gods, then your relationship with your fellows will be false. One follows the other. In Ireland both ideologies, Unionism and Nationalism, have been made into idols or false gods. When people follow a sectarian god, those who do not accept the same god are devalued and dehumanized. They become second-class citizens and injustice follows. Similar ideologies are operating today in many countries of the world.

A speaker on this theme at a Corrymeela conference compared the situation to a pyramid. At the apex is a viable political solution, accepted by both sides and enabling them to live together in peace. Below are the other parts of the pyramid on which the pinnacle rests. If the pinnacle is to be secure, the lower parts must be strong and stable, interlocking and supporting one another, otherwise they will crack and fall apart and all will tumble down.

Attitudes are all-important if our society is to be united and stable. If there are negative attitudes such as suspicion, fear and enmity, the future for everyone is dismal. But if attitudes of trust, co-operation and understanding can develop, then all things are possible. To me, this is the real arena of Corrymeela work. As Maurice Hayes, a much respected community leader and thinker, said in a recent radio programme from Derry: 'Change will come by millions of small initiatives.'

Attitudes are crucial. This, is the sphere of the peacemaker – action that seeks to change attitudes; programmes that will create trust and understanding. The prayer of St Francis, inscribed on the glass doors of the Croi, provides the complete agenda for the peacemaker:

> Where there is hatred, let me sow love,
> Where there is injury, pardon,
> Where there is doubt, faith,
> Where there is despair, hope,
> Where there is darkness, light,
> Where there is sadness, joy.

I gladly testify to the tireless efforts of a great number of individuals, groups and movements, completely apart from Corrymeela, who keep on working for a better way. I think of all those men and women, known and little known, who in their own sphere, social, political or religious, at home or school or factory or office or club or party, speak out for healing and trust. They are already doing much to change attitudes. We are glad to travel the same road with them and keep another small candle alight.

A major part of our peacemaking is simply the existence of the Centre right from the start. It has always served to keep our feet on the ground, as the continuing succession of individuals and groups who are right in the middle of the conflict continue to visit Corrymeela, sometimes just for a break and others to wrestle with their problems.

This is what Garret Fitzgerald, a former Taoiseach (Prime Minister) of the Irish Republic, wrote after a visit to Corrymeela:

> There is a contrast between the horror of a conflict based on religion as a dividing factor . . . and the living sense of Christian witness amongst so many involved in constructive work. Prayer has a new meaning in this context, above all, it must be said, in inter-denominational prayer . . . To pray thus in the present atmosphere of Northern Ireland can be an unbearably moving experience, equally for those visiting the province, as for those living and working here.

This was more succinctly put by Lord 'Billy' Blease of Cromac, a long-standing champion of Corrymeela and recently opposition spokesman on Northern Ireland in the House of Lords:

'Corrymeela means trust.'

I also remember a senior citizen's remark after his first visit in a mixed Catholic and Protestant group:

> 'This is right. This is how it should have been fifty years ago.'

At the other end of the generation spectrum there was the little six-year-old girl who was talking about 'the Troubles' to Elsbeth Bell, one of the helpers at a family week.

> 'Och,' she said, 'it's all them Praodestants – they cause the trouble.'
> Elsbeth took a deep breath and paused: 'Well, dear – I'm a Protestant.'
> The little girl, not to be put off, replied: 'No – ye're not a Proadestant at Corrymeela.'

It is impossible to do justice to the multitude of conferences, seminars, support groups, family and women's weekends, in addition to all the ecumenical meetings and the different models used in the youth programmes. But having been part of so many of them, I can see certain constant themes running through them all. Like Heinz' 57 varieties there are one or two unvarying elements in each one.

Rightly we have put much emphasis on the programmes for teenagers and young adults. They are the most vulnerable element in our society, especially at a time of massive unemployment and little hope for the future. This is the group that is most open to exploitation by the paramilitary godfathers. This poem by a Belfast teenager speaks for itself:

> God no, please
> give me violence
> again, to drown this silence
> which is killing me.
> . . . Big streets empty, full of little
> papers, cigarette ends, decaying spittle

and walking here only causes dust
to move.
. . . The big wind blows
all the dust to other footpaths,
nice and empty . . .
The snobby sun thinks he knows
it all, looking down, and he can only see
someone spitting here.

It's only me!

What then are the common ingredients of most of our programmes? There is the opportunity of living together with a mixed group of people for a few days, time to relax together in shared meals, chores, outdoor recreation, music and for some groups, discos. There is the special and liberating experience of telling 'your story' with all its hopes and fears, and at the same time listening to the other person's story. It is at such times that relationships grow. This makes the shared worship specially real.

This is one such story:

My name is Barry. I was brought up in a very strong Irish Nationalist family and am a devout Roman Catholic. I am a father and husband in my early fifties and was never involved in a community relations project until a weekend at Corrymeela seven years ago.

I do not know why I got involved. People from my own town were organizing the meeting and when asked I agreed to come. I met people from the Protestant and Unionist tradition who live in the same town as me and whom I had never talked with before. The discussions were initially very wary. Deep emotions were stirred in me, but soon, very soon, we were sharing our different views and experiences. I was overwhelmed at what came out and how people listened to one another.

At the end of the weekend I went along with the others to the short Corrymeela Community service. At the finish we were invited to say the Our Father (the Lord's Prayer). We took hands and during the prayer I began to cry into myself and at the end outwardly. I have never experienced anything like it before. It was also the first time in my life I had ever prayed with Protestants. After that weekend some of us stayed together, and we still meet and organize projects for adults and young people in the town.

In all these different programmes the emphasis is on the participants. What they learn from each other and what they decide is all-important. There are usually co-ordinators around, who will help to clarify and summarize the discussion. In addition they will help the group to identify the issues that have to be faced and the decisions that have to be taken. The main idea is not to tell those who come what they should do, but help them to decide for themselves.

How does this work out? We held a weekend for teenagers from both Catholic and Protestant schools in different parts of the country.

When Sean and Damian, from a Catholic inner-city school in Derry, agreed to come on the weekend, they feared that they would be in the minority, and no-one would be prepared to listen to their experiences and views. So they arrived wearing sweatshirts ablaze with the colours of the flag they supported, and brandishing slogans proclaiming their cause. Then, expecting to be put down by their opponents, they adopted a macho image, projecting their outlook in the most aggressive tones. Their first surprise was to discover they were not in the minority. Their second was when they learnt that many of the other Catholics present did not share their political outlook. Their biggest surprise was to discover that most of the others were prepared to accept without reaction their dress, listen calmly to what they said, and ask them why they felt that way rather than arguing back at them.

As the weekend went on their voices went down by decibels, their aggressive behaviour subsided, and they acknowledged that they were not that sure themselves about all of the most extreme positions they had proclaimed on the Friday night. Most importantly on Sunday at the final worship they said that the kind of openness and acceptance they had experienced in the group gave them hope that it was possible to pursue change through negotiation rather than force as the only way that people will consider. As a result they planned to meet together with others of the group in their home town and keep in touch and hopefully to come back to Corrymeela.

In another group of mixed adults there were two women who each had family members – one a father, the other a cousin – killed in the violence. That evening they were all telling their own experiences and these two women told of what their bereavements had cost them. But they did so without any bitterness towards the killers.

Later another member, Chuck, said:

> I have never experienced anything like that session. I live in an area where the paramilitaries who carried out both of those killings operate. I could easily have been involved in them. I have never been involved with that sort of thing myself but up till now I have quietly condoned what they did, believing this is war and those killed were legitimate targets. But listening to those two women talk about their relatives and yet somehow not bitter towards my community, I know I can't go back there and live the same way and justify to myself or anyone else the use of violence towards them.

Another Corrymeela member, Mervyn Love, led a teenage work camp at Summerfest. The young people came from all parts of

Ireland, both North and South and both Catholic and Protestant. One girl from Dublin described her experience:

> I will always be grateful to Corrymeela for offering all of us from all different walks of life and religions, just a chance to grow to love one another. Which I do believe we did, we did love one another.

Then she added:

> You all touched me so much that I put down my name to become a volunteer at Corrymeela, because I would love to be able to say that I am a part of a loving, caring group of people, and to reach out and touch people in the way that you all touched me.

One conference at Corrymeela always stays in my memory. It was a meeting of hard-line activists from both sides, indeed some with paramilitary involvement. It had been arranged by several Corrymeela friends who were in touch with these groups. There was plenty of straight and blunt discussion. Among those present was an elderly man. Through the weekend he had kept quiet and said very little. Some even began to wonder just who he was and why he was there. During the final summing-up session on Sunday evening he stood up and said: 'I suppose you have been wondering who I am, and why I am here with this English accent.' Then he paused and continued: 'Well, I am from England. I am here because of my son. He was a soldier and was killed here in the violence.' Another pause: 'I have come over because of him. I want to find out if there is anything I can do to bring peace, because that was why he came here.' There was complete silence for quite a time after he had sat down. For the first time many of them saw that the situation in the country was not black and white – the goodies and the baddies. Here was a very different approach of courage, goodness and faith that transcended the situation and suggested a better way.

A similar story comes to mind of another soldier. Nick White came to Belfast from England in 1970. His unit was placed on the 'Peace Line' in the west of the city. One of his duties was to man the observation post that had a wide vision of both the Shankill and the Ardoyne areas. From his vantage point he was able to see the children on both sides playing their games – for the most part the same games. Nick loved children and was fascinated to watch them. Then his term of service here ended and he had to move to Cyprus. But Nick could not forget about the Belfast children and finally bought himself out of the army and came back to Belfast. Here he started to work with the children. He ran a club and a disco for them. Soon the news got around that he had been a soldier. One day a gunman came into the club and shot him in front of the young people.

It is the memory of Nick White and others like him that lives on to rebuke and challenge us would-be peacemakers today!

# CHAPTER ELEVEN

# *Corrymeela begins when you leave*

*We Christians do not take Christ into the world – he is already there waiting for us to join him in his struggle.*
DIETRICH BONHOEFFER

*The journey inwards is the journey from the issues of this world towards God. It is a journey towards the mind of Christ . . . It is followed by the journey outwards back from the depths where we meet God, to the issues facing us in our everyday life.*
FROM *THE LONGEST JOURNEY*, FATHER DALRYMPLE

Every January members and friends of Corrymeela gather together for a service of dedication. The climax comes as each of us goes forward and, kneeling together, we solemnly 'surrender ourselves to the Spirit of Christ – to make us instruments of his peace'. Sometimes as I sit and wait for my turn I think of those who have knelt here and how they fulfilled this commitment.

Addie Morrow was one of our pioneers. He could be described as a man for all seasons. Not only because he is a farmer, but because of the range of his concerns and the breadth of his outlook. The family home, Streamvale Farm, about five miles from the city centre, snugly sits among the Castlereagh hills with an almost aerial view of the industrial and residential areas of Belfast, hemmed in to the north by the Antrim hills and the distant Mournes to the east. The Morrow family have initiated one of the first open farms in the province, and through it thousands of city children have a chance to share in all the variety and excitement of life on a farm.

Addie feels very strongly that, as a Christian, it is his duty to be involved in political life. In keeping with this he became a founder member of the cross-community Alliance Party which started in 1970 with the aim of getting away from sectarian politics and redirecting energy and resources to the deep social needs felt by both Catholic and Protestant, so enabling representatives of both traditions to work together for the common good of the whole country.

This has been a costly decision and has brought him a lot of personal abuse and several threats to his life and his farm. Recently he became Deputy Leader of the party and stood for the North Down seat at the Westminster Election in 1991. Addie is not in politics for any personal ambition, but because he believes that this is what discipleship means for him. In this way he feels that he can help to create a new type of politics which exists to preserve and safeguard the welfare and dignity of every citizen.

Up country in County Derry is the picturesque and well-planned town of Kilrea on the river Bann, a market town, like so many others deeply polarized by the politico-religious divide. Despite this there has been some co-operation and community activity. Four years ago the recently appointed Catholic curate approached two of the local Protestant clergy and suggested that each should invite three others from their tradition and form a small informal group to meet in different homes with the simple purpose of getting to know each other. Twelve people volunteered and the meetings take place each month. The programme is in the hands of the members, although occasionally guests are invited. Three Corrymeela people, Father Colm O'Doherty, the Rev. Dick Gordon and Dr Moreen Gordon were among the founders.

This small initiative has enabled real dialogue to take place, in which members are able to share their perceptions of each other's religion, politics and understanding of history. The group has helped in organizing a united Christmas carol service and is supporting efforts to build a local community centre.

Their courage has been severely tested by four sectarian

murders and extensive bombing in their small town. These tragic happenings were discussed openly and very fully in the group. In this way membership was both tested and cemented. A warm affection has developed as well as much fun and laughter. The meetings always close with a prayer said together. The members have kept a low profile and have not publicized the meetings. Even so its existence is now public knowledge, and many people are beginning to understand that trust and friendship can cross the deepest divide. This small group is a challenging sign for all who would like to break through the bondage of fear and create new relationships and a new spirit in a tragically divided society.

Charles Wesley, the Salvation Army, and Freedom singers of more recent times, have shown how powerful singing can be in communicating a message. One of our members, Norman Richardson, recognized this in the seventies and started 'The Corrymeela Singers'. Their purpose, through their words and music, was to capture something of the spirit of Corrymeela and peacemaking. In this way a group of talented musicians and song writers have come together and carried their message, not only throughout Ireland and Great Britain, but across Europe. With the albums they have made and the radio and television programmes in which they have performed, their challenge has literally gone round the world. Some of the members have written their own songs and music, and the best known of these is Roger Courtney's 'Pollen of Peace' which has been translated into Irish, German and Polish.

O let us spread the pollen of peace throughout our land.
Let us spread the pollen of peace throughout our land.
Let us spread the pollen of peace
And make all conflict cease.
Let us spread the pollen of peace throughout our land.

O Christ has sown the seeds of love;
O Christ has launched the wingèd dove.
Let us make the flower grow,

And let the people know,
That Christ has sown the seeds of love.

All it needs is our love to make it grow;
All it needs is our hopefulness to show
And tell those that are filled with fear
That the Prince of Peace is here.
All it needs is our love to let it grow.

Peacemaking is often a costly and dangerous task, as another of our memberes discovered. Mary Healy lives in Armagh where she is employed as a secretary. Mary is married to Gus and they have three grown-up children. Though this ancient city is the ecclesiastical capital of Ireland, and has two cathedrals and close links with St Patrick, the patron saint of Ireland, it too has its sadness. The area has been referred to as 'the murder triangle' and has a tragic list of victims. Feelings between the two communities have never been easy.

Beneath Mary's warm and gentle exterior lie very deep convictions and the determination to carry them through. She felt that something had to be done about the continuing violence. With some others she decided to form an interdenominational peace group. The next step was the decision to go public in order to reach as many people as possible. They set about planning a Peace Rally in the centre of Armagh on Saturday 9th October 1976. Mary as organizer notified the press giving her name, address and phone number, as contact person.

Abusive and threatening phone calls came thick and fast, and the climax came when a two-page letter arrived from a paramilitary group with a fierce condemnation of the march, and ending with these chilling sentences: 'I must inform you that if you proceed with this ridiculous march planned for the 9th October in Armagh we will do all in our power to disrupt the marchers. We shall also single out marchers for assassination, and I personally will execute you or a member of your family.'

The letter concluded with these words written in capitals: 'THIS IS NO IDLE THREAT.'

What was Mary to do? She discussed it with Gus. It was a distressing time for them, as they realized the dangers to themselves and their children. They had never had any experience like this. What was right for them? For several agonizing days they thought about it. Then Mary knew she must go on, and in her decision she had the full support of Gus.

Mary described to me what she went through in those days, and how finally she sat down and prayed: ' 'My God, I give you my house, my family, my husband and myself.' Slowly, as I sat in the quiet of my room, I was aware of a great sense of peace within me. I began to think of the person who had written the letter, and I forgave him. Because through him I had found a new way of life which otherwise I would not have had.'

The rally went on as planned. There was a massive response as they gathered at the Market House. Every denomination was represented and there was no opposition and no violence.

Peacemaking means that we often have to face up to the most divisive problems. One such is the segregated school system in Northern Ireland. Thus 98 per cent of Catholic children are in Catholic schools, while 99.5 per cent of Protestant children are in state or other non-Catholic schools. While there are deeply rooted historical reasons for this, to me it becomes ever clearer that in such a polarized society as ours separate schooling has got to be challenged as a luxury we cannot afford.

The late James Young, a popular Belfast comedian and satirist, expresses the concrete everyday reality of what this separation means to the ordinary child in our country, in one of his monologues.

Davy Shaw, the seven-year-old Protestant child, asks his father:

'Why can't I go to school with Pat O'Shea?
Pat's school is just around the corner
And mine is more than half a mile away.'
'You can't go to his school,'

His father answered.
'I've told you that a thousand times and more.'
'But what's the reason, Da?' Wee Davy asked him.
'In Catholic schools is two plus two not four?
Do they not learn reading and spelling
Geometry and geography like us?'
'You just don't understand,' his father told him.
'It's history that causes all the fuss.'
'But I'm not learning history yet,' said Davy.
'And if I was you know what I could do?
I could learn the other things they teach them,
And then I could learn my history from you.'
'You're not to go to his school.'
His father told him.
'Don't let me find you next nor near the place.'
'But Pat's my friend,' he told him.
And the tears were burning black furrows in his face.

But there are signs of new thinking and change.

In 1977 the All Children Together movement was started. For the most part it was a pressure group of parents who believed they should have the right to decide how their children should be educated. It was not an attack on the current system of separate schooling, but rather that they, the parents, should have the choice of integrated education.

Dorothy Wilson, a Corrymeela member, has been very much involved in this campaign, and was one of the founders of the Mill Strand Primary School in Portrush, County Antrim. She is the joint author of a booklet on Integrated Education. In this she describes the purpose of these new schools:

> to allow Protestant and Catholic children in Northern Ireland to be educated together without becoming any less Protestant or any less Catholic . . . There is a long-standing, violent conflict in Northern Ireland, and the two sides in the conflict often know very little

about each other. Part of the underlying philosophy of the new schools is the view that, if children went to school together, some of the mutual ignorance might be dissolved . . . It is hoped that the attitudes acquired at school will also affect their parents and the rest of their families.

Two Corrymeela members, Maura and Edmund Kiely, live in Dundonald an eastern suburb of Belfast. They had two children: Gerard and Mary. Mary has now qualified as a doctor but Gerard, their student son, was shot dead on the steps of a chapel in south Belfast. Maura describes what took place:

It happened on 9th February, 1975 on a Sunday evening. Gerard was a first-year student at Queen's University, studying economics, and he was almost nineteen. He was staying in the Queen's Halls of Residence, though normally he came home each weekend, and he always went back on the Sunday evening. That particular weekend he had been studying for an examination, so he decided to stay on at the university. We saw him there on the Saturday and left about 10:30 p.m. As I left I said: 'Don't forget to go to Mass tomorrow morning.' He left me to the door and said: 'I'll go to St Brigid's in the evening.' That was the first Sunday he did not go to church with us.

Apparently he left his room at five to seven. He was dead at 7:30. Two gunmen were waiting as the congregation filed out and they fired into the crowd indiscriminately. The road lights were broken, and the grounds of the church were completely dark. So they fired against the lights of the church as the doors were opened . . .

I was numbed. I nearly lost my faith. I could not understand why God had allowed such a dastardly act to take place on the threshold of His church, especially when Gerard was performing his religious duties. I was very bitter. Easter was coming and then I began to realize . . . suddenly something just hit me, that God had chosen me for some reason or another to suffer. I did not know why, but I believed that God had given me this cross and that I would have to bear it. If we were going to remain bitter we were going to destroy ourselves completely as a family. From then on I began to accept his death and it was my faith and upbringing that pulled me through . . .

When I decided that the bitterness would have to go, something inside me kept saying: 'Go and meet someone else who has lost a son.' It was like a voice telling me what to do. Night and day it kept at me. At that point I met a priest and told him about it. He said: 'Maura, why don't you start something?' I hadn't a clue. He offered to give me all the help he could. So I went home and thought about it and decided to go ahead.

I compiled a list of names and addresses from newspapers. Then I went to them personally. I did not write. I had been advised not to phone. I might have started on the wrong footing. So on the very first night I left my house with four names of people to visit. It was pelting with rain. I remember it well. I got to only one house. I arrived at 7:30 and left at midnight. At the first meeting we held, we had thirty people. It was marvellous though we were too many.

We developed into something like a support group and we began to meet regularly . . . The people went home liberated. We talked about all kinds of things, the price of meat, shopping, fashion, holidays, anything . . .

At the beginning I said to someone we would have the relatives of innocent victims, and I was told: 'How

can YOU tell who was innocent and who was not?'
Of course that was right. I should not presume to
judge anyone. The fact that someone has committed
an awful crime does not mean that they haven't asked
God for forgiveness. There is no point in believing in
God if you don't believe in forgiveness from God. So
maybe the boy who shot Gerard has already made his
peace with God . . .

Thirteen years ago Peter Tennent with Valerie, his wife, very
gently and unobtrusively slipped into the life of Corrymeela.
Peter is a member of the Society of Friends and has worked in
peacemaking in several parts of the world including China. So
they decided that they would leave their wooded hill farm in
Scotland and come and work with Corrymeela. What a gift he
has been to our community! Before he arrived Corrymeela was
just a bare, wind-swept and exposed site on eight acres of open
land with the house at one corner. The only signs of growth
apart from the grass were a few escallonia bushes close to the
house. Experts had told us that little else would grow on such
an open position. But Peter quietly researched possibilities, he
consulted experts and then slowly and systematically began to
plant the trees that could survive. Gradually sycamore, ash, silver
fir, lodge pole pine and hornbeam appeared. Many of them
perished but Peter persisted and now five acres of the area are
covered with flourishing trees. How vastly they have changed
the whole atmosphere of Corrymeela, knitting all the buildings
and open spaces into a very pleasant and intimate unity. Peter
has taught us all a new appreciation of the natural world and how
we should treasure and preserve our beautiful environment.

But Peter is not only the man who plants trees. He has brought
his patience and thoroughness into a very different and equally
demanding activity. Since its foundation in 1981 he has worked
very closely with the Committee on the Administration of
Justice. This independent organization works for 'the highest
standards in the administration of justice'. It has focused on such

divisive subjects as prisons, a Bill of Rights, policing, emergency laws and aspects of social legislation. Peter's special interest has been in policing and he has written four pamphlets on this subject.

Like tree planting on an open headland, this is slow and unspectacular work, but it is a vital component of peacemaking. If we ignore it, we deserve the reproach of Jeremiah to the false prophets: 'They have healed the wound of my people lightly,' saying "Peace, peace," when there is no peace.'

The story of another member, Mervyn Love, is very different. Mervyn was living a normal quiet life as a civil servant. He had been brought up in a strongly Protestant Loyalist area, and when militant Republican groups became active, he believed with many of his friends that the security of the state was at risk. So when Protestant paramilitary activities began he became involved.

This lasted from 1970 to '74. Eventually he became tired of it all and disillusioned, as he knew that many were simply using the situation for their own ends. He decided he had had enough and finally left. But that was not the end for him. Some time later the security forces arrested him and he was charged on the grounds of paramilitary activities and offences, and eventually sent to prison to serve a long sentence.

This was a most chastening time for him, as he began to think about his future and what he was hoping to do with his life. He began to see through many of his presuppositions. This led to great despondency and disillusionment. One day he got talking to a visiting clergyman and told him his story. He was very impressed by the man, because he listened and did not condemn or judge. He simply said: 'I believe you are searching desperately for something in life. I believe that if you read this you may find the answer.'

> It was the Gospel of St John. I read it and reread it and I became intrigued by the verse: 'Greater love hath no man than this, that a man lay down his life

for his friends'. I thought, 'Who would I give my life
for?' It was precious few.

I went on to read about this Man who had been
viciously tortured and still could say on the Cross,
'Father, forgive them.' You know I couldn't grasp it,
but I knew it was powerful. I wanted to plug into that
and I decided at that point that I would follow the
Christian path. The rest of my friends said 'crazy' or
'he's working a fast one to get out, it'll last a week,
three weeks, three months or at most nine months'.
Well that was in 1974 and it's still as real today. I
decided at that point that my life had to change . . .
I decided that I would study, that I would take a
degree. The prison said this was impossible, that it
had never been done before. That was a challenge
and I did do it.

I was eventually released after five years in Long
Kesh. One of the first things I did was to attend a
conference at Corrymeela on the effects of long-term
imprisonment. As a result of this someone at
Corrymeela said to me: 'We think you need time, you
need space, you need neutral ground, you need
people around you. Come up here and stay with us
for a week. If you want to talk to people, they're here
to listen. If you don't want to talk to people, nobody
will make any judgments, nobody will be quizzing
you, take your time.'

Gradually things began to work out. Two Corrymeela members
were organizing an experimental scheme for young offenders in
a large house close to Ballycastle. Mervyn felt that if he got a
chance he would have something to give in such an
establishment. He applied and was taken on as a volunteer on
a trial basis.

For four and a half years I worked with these young lads and I know for a fact that I was instrumental in preventing quite a few of them being involved in paramilitary activity . . . But more than that, it was bringing across to them that violence is violence irrespective of party labels. They had to learn to come to terms with themselves and their communities and discover how they'd go back and live in those communities.

I also started to work at Corrymeela with young people who abused alcohol and drugs and participated in glue sniffing; with intimidated families: single-parent families; very poor families; prisoners' families; paramilitaries' families; Protestant and Catholic groups; victims of the violence. I began to realize the tremendous work that was going on there with workers and community members going out into areas, trying to bring people together on neutral ground for a chance to explore with each other, to talk to each other, to see what were the suspicions . . . I have worked with so many groups. I have seen the tears, I have seen the shock, I have seen the myths blown away and people begin to realize: 'We are people on this earth and we NEED to live together. Whether we kill each other or not, somebody has got to say enough is enough. I can't take any more. I just want to live. I just want to get on with my neighbour.'

We in Corrymeela, as reconcilers, have to face and overcome the many emotions such groups bring with them: fear, suspicion, bigotry, prejudice and hurts, to name but a few. We face criticism for almost any reason your imagination can create for you. However, I believe it is worth the effort. I have seen the results. I have experienced the joy of divides being crossed, barriers broken down, attitudes changed and firm new bridges built. Most of all I have seen my own transformation from my old life to the new creation as the inner hope and belief that through faith in God and in the reconciling power of Jesus Christ, change can come about. It is a constant reminder to me that reconcilation in our society is a real and viable proposition, but, of course, there is a sting – it is costly. But to try and go on without being reconciled one to the other is eventually even more costly.

These different stories about peacemakers are only a few of many that could be told. But they remind us that peace cannot be confined to our private individual experience, but also concerns all of life. It is a public matter and deals with the realities of everyday life in our society and world.

Peace with God and our own forgiveness and reconciliation are vital, but just a start. Jesus is emphatic about that. He tells us that if we love him, we will keep his commandments and seek first his kingdom. In the little sketches he gives us of that kingdom, he leaves us in no doubt. These demand action, not just contemplation; obedience, not just prayer; discipleship, not just admiration.

Blessed are the peacemakers, for they shall be called the children of God.
Blessed are they that hunger for justice for they shall be satisfied.

# CHAPTER TWELVE

# *Hope*

*For you alone are my hope, Lord.* PSALM 71:5

*He's got the whole world in his hand.* TRADITIONAL SPIRITUAL

I am very often asked: 'Have you got any hope for the future of our country?' Usually the questioner is expecting a political answer – some model to hold together our different traditions. For me there is only one answer: 'I am hopeful because I believe in God.' I know that will sound trite and smug to many people, but for me that is the place where I have to begin, and that is at the heart of what Corrymeela tries to do.

Political processes and choices are necessary. To formulate these, there has to be debate and bargaining about social, cultural and economic issues. But, as John Morrow reminds us from time to time: 'We've got to dig deeper.' At a Corrymeela Conference an eminent academic was giving a paper on 'The Economic Problems of Northern Ireland.' He spoke about mass unemployment; the diminishing investment from outside, and the continuing destruction of life and property through terrorist activity. As he concluded, he took us all by surprise by changing his line of argument and very urgently speaking of the overwhelming need for trust and co-operation. There is no other way forward. If such could happen, then new thinking and new answers would be possible. Professor John White, writing as a political scientist, came to a similar conclusion:

> The task for statesmanship is to devise arrangements whereby the opposing sets of anxieties and grievances can be assuaged.

How then are the anxieties and grievances, the fears and the enmities, to be addressed? To me the answer can come in a renewal and rediscovery of the Christian hope, which is shared, at least in name, by the vast majority of people in this island. But many have accepted the view, shallow and uninformed as it is, that religion itself is the real problem. After all, one bad baker does not stop people eating bread. This raises the most basic question we can ask ourselves: 'What sort of a God do we worship?' Because our values and attitudes depend on our answer.

In Ireland we have interned God in our own traditions. He has been reduced to a tribal deity – the God of the Protestants or the God of the Catholics. We have tried to tame and domesticate him and fit him into our particular formation of the Faith. We have privatized God and used him as a means to further our own interests and those of our tradition.

One day Kathleen was showing a lady round Corrymeela. She was well educated and an active member of her Protestant Church. As they were passing through the different buildings they met a volunteer worker, who explained what her job was. As they were moving on, the visitor said to her: 'May God bless you in your work.' Casually Kathleen explained that she was one of our Catholic volunteers. The lady stopped in her tracks, looked at her in dismay and exclaimed: 'Oh, I should not have said that.'

'Why not?' replied Kathleen.

'But their God is different from ours!'

To me the greatest tragedy is that many people in each tradition cannot accept the other as Christian. This is the first barrier that Corrymeela tries to break down.

On another occasion I was looking after two visitors who had come in for lunch. They had no idea what Corrymeela was about, so I gave them a very brief outline of our aims and programme and how we sought to bring together people from both sides. When I spoke about having Catholics and Protestants together, there was quite a pause and then the man said: 'Yes, I do believe in mixing with Catholics – in order to convert them.'

Now it was my turn to pause. Then I replied: 'Well, I would

have had problems three weeks ago, when I had lunch with Mother Teresa of Calcutta. Just where would you start to try to convert her, for I have never met anyone with such a Christ-like spirit?'

He did not reply, but I could see that it had given him some food for thought. To me it is all-important to understand the God to whom we commit our lives. We cannot tie him down to our tradition or our formulation of the faith. He is King of Kings and Lord of Lords. We believe that the nearer we get to him the closer we will be to each other.

This is why our Corrymeela liturgy is so central, holding us all, both Catholics and Protestants, together:

> Christ is our Peace
> He has broken down the hostility between us.
> There is neither Jew nor Greek, slave nor free,
> male or female.
> We are one in you.
> . . . . . . . .
> We are Your body,
> And are members of one another.
> We are a community of the Holy Spirit,
> Called to be witnesses of God's love.

There are large numbers of people in the country who deplore sectarianism, but are unwilling to do anything about it. They are content to ignore it and even use their religion as a means of escape from any sort of political or social involvement.

While saints introspect, burly sinners run the world.

Another subtle method of evading responsibility is constantly to blame others. We call it 'scapegoating'. This has become almost the normal pattern for our daily politics. We can either scapegoat the 'terrorist' or 'the British army' or 'the police'. Or more simply, depending on our mood or stance, we castigate 'the Catholics', 'Dublin', 'the Brits' or 'the Prods'.

Sometimes there is an even more subtle approach, frequently by churchpeople who look at reconciliation as an extra-curricular option, a specialized activity which you can take up or not according to your inclination. It is often implied in some church circles that if you want to be involved in peacemaking in the community you should go to Corrymeela or some other peace organization. But is peacemaking not what the Gospel and the churches are all about? God is a God of peace. His business is peacemaking. This is his thing. His peace is not only a vertical one between us and God, but also horizontal, between person and person, church and church, tradition and tradition. To be a follower of Christ, we are called 'to seek peace and pursue it.'

Friday 21st July 1972 has taken its place in our Irish history. It is known as 'Bloody Friday'. On that day the Provisional IRA set off twenty-six explosions in Belfast. Eleven people were killed and 130 injured, many seriously. Seven were killed at the Oxford Street bus station and four at a shopping centre on the Cavehill Road in north Belfast. One of these was a fourteen-year-old schoolboy, Stephen Parker. He lost his life as he went back to a shop to warn the shoppers about the bomb. His father is the Rev. Joe Parker, a Church of Ireland minister, and at that time Chaplain to the Seamen's Mission in York Street close to the docks.

No one who saw Joe being interviewed on television will ever forget what he said. He described the bombing and how he had been called to the hospital to identify his son. The only way he was able to recognize him was when a conjuring trick was found in one of his trouser pockets. He knew that Stephen always carried this with him.

Joe did not withdraw in his grief. He knew that he had to speak out, as he realized the blasphemy and sacrilege of what had happened, not only to Stephen, but to so many other innocent victims. His suffering sharpened his perception and he felt compelled to express what he felt. He became an authentic prophet, using every chance through the media and press as well as peace vigils all over the province to bring home to the country the need for a vast change in attitude and commitment.

Like the great prophets, he proclaimed his message right at the heart of the city when he went on a fast in front of the City Hall. What a striking figure he made as he stood there tall and straight, with his black hair, deep-set eyes and face emaciated with grief! His voice was compelling in its conviction and urgency. I stood there and watched him as he pled for peace and reconciliation. I listened to the abuse hurled at him. Some even mocked him about his son's death. In that moment I understood something more of another Son's death at Calvary.

Like the prophets, he was not content with words, he dramatized his message. He created a movement, 'Witness for Peace', which not only gave much-needed support to those who, like Joe, had lost a member of their family but, in addition, it galvanized many into action for peace in the country.

Joe's message was a simple one. It was a call to repentance. When I heard him speak, I knew that this word was not an obsolete theological cliché, but a clear uncompromising demand that we should all change our direction and turn round in our thinking and attitudes. His message was for everyone, because we are all in this, not only by what we have done but also by what we have not done. Although Joe has moved away from this country to Vancouver, his words, example and courage continue to inspire many people in the search for peace.

It is not easy at times to remain hopeful as the grim cycle of tit-for-tat killings continues from day to day. There is much political pessimism, and many commentators continue to 'blow out the candle at the end of the tunnel'. I know that underneath, there is a great power struggle, indeed, a battle for the soul of our country. On the one hand there are those who talk exclusively of the interests and victory of 'our people' or 'ourselves alone'. There are others who want to include 'my people' with 'your people'. There are those whose sole argument is the bomb and the bullet, and those who also want change, but through negotiation, compromise and partnership.

I believe there is hope even in the difficult political field. It is bound to be slow and tortuous, given the deep shadows of past events. There is a new desire among most politicians, both north and south, for political movement. At least political talks have taken place and more are on the agenda. This is a new thing in the vexed history of this island. Traditional attitudes in the main political parties, both north and south, are becoming more realistic, and there is a very widespread desire for a settlement that will do justice to both traditions.

I am even more sure that there is an increasing groundswell among the ordinary people. For the first time in our history there are not only occasional individuals who crusade for peace, but over the last ten to twenty years more and more new organizations and pressure groups have come into existence. These are made up of multitudes of people who long for peace, and are determined to work for it. This is a new phenomenon and it will not go away. I often quote Matthew Arnold's lines in 'La grande Chartreuse': 'Wandering between two worlds, one dead, the other powerless to be born'. There is no doubt in my mind that the old order is passing and the other may yet be powerless, but it is there and it will not go away.

The very names of many recently-established organizations speak for themselves. We have: ACT – All Children Together, PACE – Protestant and Catholic Encounter, EMU – Education for Mutual Understanding, the Peace People and multitudes of other cross-community efforts. A significant example of this change of mood and heart-cry for peace is Initiative '92. Any person or group who wished to put forward a submission about the future of Northern Ireland was invited to do so. Over 600 submissions have been passed to the Opsahl Commission of seven eminent people from Britain, Ireland and Europe. Many outsiders who come to this country are amazed at its vibrance and resilience and this vast network of cross-community organizations. All this in spite of the long years of violence and destruction. These bodies have steadily worked to build social, sporting, cultural, economic and ecumenical links across the divide. Such bridges have quietly appeared unheralded and often unnoticed. They articulate the voice of an ever-increasing number of people who want to live and work peacefully together.

I love to watch the Belfast Marathon which takes place each May Day and passes near our home. To me it is a picture of the society that Northern Ireland can become, where the emphasis is not on victory or rivalry, but on running side by side, sharing the ordeals and struggles, supporting and encouraging one another. It is an annunciation of a true community, where there is no 'us' or 'them', but all of us running together in confidence and hope, a sign of what the good Lord wants our society to become.

Another very different image comes to mind. It is of a vast 5000–strong group of schoolchildren and teenagers. They walked down the Ormeau Road in torrential rain, where on 5th February 1992, two terrorists had rushed into Sean Graham's betting shop and gunned down five men just because they were believed to be Catholic. The procession passed the shop and proceeded to a mass meeting in the Botanic Gardens where the leaders spoke out against what had happened and pleaded with politicians and community leaders to find a better way for everyone.

Then there has been the long-term constant witness of the Irish Council of Churches with all the difficult parts of its work in Church Unity and Peace Education, the Irish School of Ecumenics, the Christian Renewal Centre at Rostrevor, and more recently the work of the Cornerstone, Columbanus, and Columba Communities and multitudes of ongoing joint services, conferences and prayer groups.

The supreme value of all these organizations, both religious and secular, has above all been in the creation of new relationships. This is the real gateway to hope and it is an option open to everyone. Looking back over the Corrymeela years the supreme thing for me has been the number of people that have met and come to know, value and trust each other. Through friendships many have been immeasurably enriched in self-knowledge, wider understanding and in personal faith. So often even after the most impressive conferences people have said: 'It wasn't the formal speeches that were important to me, but the chance to meet and get to know so and so.'

This came home very powerfully three years ago when in March 1989 Bishop David Sheppard and Archbishop Derek Worlock, the Protestant and Catholic leaders of Liverpool, visited Belfast. The meeting in Queen's University was in the form of a dialogue, giving a fascinating and at times humorous picture of their work together in a city so like Belfast. But to those who were present, it was not what they said, important as it was, that mattered most. Rather it was that these two church leaders from the different traditions were obviously so much at one, and overarching their differences there was a deep trust and friendship. In this they made Christian reconciliation alive and visible, showing a pattern of utter simplicity that could be duplicated over and over again.

It is this multiplication of relationships across the barriers that gives me great hope. It is the supreme gift that Corrymeela brings to its members and friends. I think of it especially when we share our worship together. It is a family reunion, when I meet my brothers and sisters again after the centuries-old dispute with all its bitterness and pain. It is these special meetings that make Corrymeela so important to us all. It is a gift, a very special gift, given to us by the Spirit – the one who draws us together, the go-between God. I cannot estimate how greatly my life has been enriched by so many such friendships.

A very important relationship for me has been with Father Tony Farquhar, whom I had met when he was one of the Catholic chaplains at Queen's University. Since then he has become Auxiliary Bishop of Down and Connor. I have learnt much from him: what his faith means to him, his dedication and spirituality, his deep love and concern for young people, his zest for life be it folk music or football, his lovely sense of humour and the sincerity of his friendship. I have seen the price he pays for his vocation and the strength of his discipline. Nor can I forget the way in which he accepted me as a friend and a brother in Christ.

This acceptance did not mean that he expected me to give up my convictions. Nor did I think he should surrender his. We accepted each other with our differences. I have still many problems with his tradition and he with mine. Even so, we can accept each other as followers of the one Lord and face our differences in the spirit of trust and openness. Hence the importance of real meeting; this means risk-taking, finding common ground and being willing to share our lives, our interests, our concerns and our faith. In this way we learn to grow together.

On the evening of Good Friday 1988, two Christian Communities, Cornerstone and Columba House, organized a Peace Walk in West Belfast. This is an area that has suffered continual violence and killing since the Troubles began, resulting in the erection of a 'Peace Wall'. This supposedly protects homes and families on one side from the troublemakers on the other side. The Walk was a response to the terrible events in Gibraltar, the Milltown Cemetery and Andersonstown which had filled the whole community with a deep sense of fear and anxiety about what lay ahead.

About two thousand of us set out from Mackie's factory on the Springfield Road. It was a silent walk and some groups carried peace banners. Our apprehension was intensified as we learnt of threats from a paramilitary group. The first stage took us through the Catholic area where we were warmly received. The people stood at their doors and applauded and some joined in the walk. I was deeply moved when we suddenly came to the Peace Wall. A door in this had been specially opened so that we could pass through. Suddenly the words on one of the banners became very much alive for us all:

> Christ is our peace who has broken down the middle
> wall of separation.

On the other side there were many who supported our walk and applauded but others were very hostile and some stones and eggs were thrown. Several young adults tried to break through the walk and attack us but they were stopped by the police.

We finally entered the Woodvale Park on the Shankill Road. Here a short service had been planned but had to be curtailed, when a sudden and heavy shower of rain descended on us. Then as we were leaving the park, feeling wet and cold, suddenly the clouds began to break apart and a very sharp clear rainbow appeared, spanning the whole city – an unforgettable sign of hope that the love and mercy of God overarched our city and country and each one of us, both Catholic and Protestant.

# CHAPTER THIRTEEN

# *Forgiveness*

*Forgive us the wrongs we have done, as we forgive the wrongs
others have done us . . . For if you forgive others the wrongs they
have done you, your Father in heaven will also forgive you.*
MATTHEW 6:12,14

*And when you stand praying, forgive what you have against
anyone, so that your Father in heaven will forgive your sins.*
MARK II:25

'*One of my guards came to me one day and asked, 'Do you
remember those first six months?' I remembered only too well!
They had been horrible, cruel, and this man was the worst. 'Now,'
he said, 'Abouna, dear Father, do you forgive me?' I looked at
him. 'Saeed,' I said, 'I hated. I need your forgiveness.' At that
moment I was free.'* FATHER LAWRENCE JENCO, HOSTAGE IN BEIRUT –
SPEAKING AT THE "BEYOND HATE" CONFERENCE IN DERRY

Love and forgiveness are the only weapons the Gospel offers.
They were the only ones Christ used and the only power he
exerted.

Among the final words he used on the cross were, 'Father
forgive them.' Here we stand at the heart of the Gospel. As John
Baker reminds us: 'The crucified Christ is the only accurate
picture of God the world has ever seen.' The God we see there
is vulnerable because love, if it is real, is vulnerable. Every one
of us in our own relationships, as parent or friend, knows how
true this is.

I shall never forget an incident that happened at Corrymeela
some years ago. Mother Teresa had come to participate in our
Summerfest. Naturally, it was impossible for more than a few
people to meet her personally, so it was arranged that small

groups with special needs would have that privilege. One such group was a bus-load of Belfast mothers with young children returning from a prison visit to Magilligan, some seventy miles from Belfast. They were all exhausted, the mothers feeling the pain of their isolation as prisoners' wives, the children weary after the long journey. The door opened and Mother Teresa stood there studying each face silently. Then she spoke. 'You mothers', she said, 'are very privileged.' Astonishment registered on every face. 'You are able,' she continued, 'to share the pain of Our Lady. You have to watch your dearest one suffer and do nothing about it.' Then raising her hand with an emphatic gesture she added: 'And you must smile five times a day. It is good for the children.'

It is in our weakness, vulnerability and brokenness, that God – the vulnerable God – meets us, heals and forgives us and opens up a new life. This has become more and more real to me at Corrymeela as I meet those who, even in the darkest hour of their own brokenness and suffering have been able to forgive those responsible. As I meet and talk to them I meet God in them and understand forgiveness in a new way and see how even in their suffering, God is able to use it for good.

There is Maura Kiely and her Cross group and all the support and encouragement it has given to many who have also lost a loved one. I think of Hylda Armstrong, Shaun's mother, and of how her refusal to hate and her gentle and loving witness in the cause of peacemaking all over the world, have inspired us all. Then there is Gordon Wilson of Enniskillen and his willingness to forgive those who had killed his daughter, Marie, a young nurse. No one will ever forget the radio interview he gave just after her death. He said: 'I bear no ill will. I bear no grudge. She was a great wee lassie. She loved her profession. She's in heaven now. We will meet again.'

Mary Gregory lives in Andersonstown in West Belfast. She has seven children. Her husband, Malachy, was a post office engineer. One day a gunman rushed into his office and shot him dead. It turned out to be a case of mistaken identity. Later at a

Corrymeela conference, Mary fell into conversation with a man who was sitting beside her. She discovered that he had been a terrorist but had changed his ways. Then he asked about her life. 'My husband was shot dead,' she began. The man blanched. 'Tell me when and where,' he begged her and she told him. 'Thank God', he said, 'It wasn't me.' 'If it only had been you', she replied, 'I could have forgiven you.'

How much we have to learn from these people who have been to the frontiers of human sorrow, suffering and loss. Yet they have been able to come back and forgive and not seek retaliation or revenge. In the depths of their suffering and brokenness they show us the power of Christian forgiveness. In them we see that in the end the love and forgiveness that come from Christ are stronger than hate. In their attitude they are offering us all, the way out of the cycle of violence and endless retaliation, a new way in which politics can become the art of living together with all our differences, and in which compromise and generosity can play their part.

Christ's words, 'Forgive us . . . as we forgive others' are inescapable for us all. If we are unwilling to forgive, and that includes forgiving ourselves, then we cannot be forgiven. I believe the real love triangle is between God, ourselves and others. When I know that God forgives and accepts me, then I can forgive and accept myself. When that happens I am able to forgive others. To me it is a power circuit of love and forgiveness. God receives and forgives me, but if I don't pass on that acceptance and forgiveness to those from whom I am separated, then the circuit is broken.

'How can you say, I love God and hate your brother?'

Forgiveness is a central part of the Gospel and of all our liturgies and worship. It is crystal clear whether we be Catholic or Protestant, charismatic, evangelical or liberal. It is the central part of the Mass, of Holy Communion, the Lord's Supper and the Breaking of Bread. Every Christian denomination sooner or later joins in the Lord's prayer: 'Forgive us our trespasses as we forgive those who trespass against us'. How can we receive the

Lord's Body and Blood unless we are willing to make a new relationship with our enemies? The Masai in Kenya dramatically illustrate this, for when there is a disagreement or conflict in the tribe, the Eucharist cannot take place.

There are many outside or on the fringes of our churches, and they have the right to challenge us to be what we claim to be, the Body of Christ, the true alternative society that lives by forgiveness and love, the people who are called to make Christ visible. This is the challenge Corrymeela people live with each day. In our Prayer Guide, members use this prayer:

> We commit ourselves to each other – in joy and sorrow.
> We commit ourselves to all who share our belief in reconciliation – to support and stand by them.
> We commit ourselves to the way of peace – in thought and deed.
> We commit ourselves to You as our guide and friend.

I believe that Corrymeela was given to us. The years have taught us that we are not self-sufficient. The Spirit has guided and kept us through all our blindness and failure. We have been given those little annunciations, in those who have come to us and given their love and service, and in the support that comes to us from near and far.

We do not see ourselves as an alternative church. Most of us are active members in our own denominations. But we do believe, as Tullio Vinay said at the start, that we are to be 'question marks to the Church', that we all together find new ways of being the Church.

At the heart of our vision is Christ as Lord over everything, both the private and public sectors of our lives. We know also that he is the servant and in our loyalty to him we reach out to the hungry, the thirsty, the stranger, the naked, the sick and the prisoners.

Above all, we know that all we have to give is the forgiveness and love of God. We know that we can only forgive as we are forgiven and only love because we are first loved. It is in living that out in all our relationships and all our programmes, that Corrymeela will live.

One Sunday afternoon on 24th November 1991, the Croi was packed. Some were sitting on chairs, others on the floor on cushions. We were gathered in a circle round a small table and on it was a Celtic Cross of bog oak; beside it was an open Bible and a vase of flowers. We had come for the closing act of a conference on 'the Healing of Memory'. It was a service of Holy Communion. The weekend was for Friends of Corrymeela, and people had come from all over Ireland, as well as from England and Scotland. In our meetings we had been sharing our memories of past events. Many told stories of great sadness, of relatives and friends who had died or been killed in recent happenings; others spoke of the fear in which they lived in the present time.

John Morrow, in his short homily, spoke about the different ways in which we can remember, how we can dwell on the hurts, the betrayals and the injustices to such an extent that they imprison us and block our way to new relationships. Often we can be selective and avoid the negative and unpleasant parts of our own history.

But here round this table we learn to listen to each other's stories. We learn to understand what has shaped us. And as we listen to each other's hurt memories, we learn that we can understand and forgive each other. In this way we become free and released from the bitter memories of the past. Forgiveness is both remembering and forgetting.

This is why the Sacrament of Holy Communion is the most important place of remembering. Because here we rediscover our most basic identity, as children of God, and as brothers and sisters in Christ. All our other identities are put into perspective here. In meeting Christ at this table, we recall who we really are and we also remember afresh God's generous love towards us, and his forgiving love which sets us free and makes it possible for us to set each other free.

These were the prayers of confession used in the service:

'As an *English Quaker* I ask forgiveness from God and you, my brothers and sisters, for the way my people have hurt you so much in the past and are still hurting you. I ask your forgiveness for the decisions of the past which gave away your land and divided your beautiful country. For the miscarriage of justice. For decisions made for you and not with you. For the indifference to your pain. For the insensitivity to your feelings. For arrogance. For not appreciating enough the richness of your culture and way of life. In short, for not loving you enough.'

An *Irish Catholic.* 'Lord you have insisted that we love our neighbours as ourselves. Often we in the South are tempted to turn our backs on the conflict in the North, while at the same time laying claim in our Constitution to the whole island. Inasmuch as we have neglected the people of the North, both Catholic and Protestant, and are often ignorant of their problems, we ask your forgiveness. Help us also to relate to our British neighbours in a growing spirit of healing and mutual forgiveness. Lord hear us.'

A *Northern Irish Catholic.* 'John said to Jesus: "Teacher, we saw a man casting out demons in your name, and we forbade him because he was not following us."

'Jesus said: "Do not forbid him, for no one who does a mighty work in my name will be able soon after to speak evil of me. For he that is not against us, is for us.'

'I humbly ask forgiveness for our insensitive use of the words "non-Catholic" which would seem to label you as second-class or inferior Christians.

'I ask forgiveness of you, my brothers and sisters, and of Almighty God, for the murder and brutality being inflicted by the pursuance through violent means, of a legitimate political aim.'

A *Northern Protestant.* 'O God, you are the Father of our Lord Jesus Christ. In your presence we Protestants ask our Catholic brothers and sisters to forgive us:

For all the ways you have suffered from us and our forebears in the past.

For callous cruelty, brutal evictions, tragic emigrations, for continual discrimination and the Penal Laws – Forgive us.

For refusing to listen and understand your story, your hurts, your fears, sorrows and tears.

For all the ridicule, scorn, cruel wit and careless words.

For all the unwillingness to understand and appreciate your tradition and your culture.

For the times we passed you by on the other side and refused to stop to talk and to care – O Lord forgive us.

Father forgive us. Heal our wounds, heal our memories and make us whole.

Unite us by your spirit that we may become your family, forgiven and forgiving.'

The service ended as together we said the Prayer of St Francis:

Lord make me a channel of your peace:

. . . . . . . . . . . . . . . . . . . . . . . . . . . .

For it is in giving we receive,
It is in pardoning that we are pardoned,
It is in dying that we are born to eternal life.

There is a recently written parable about the Last Day which reminds me of Jesus' story of the shepherd who had a hundred sheep and loses one of them. He leaves the ninety-nine and goes after the strayed one until it is found.

There is singing and dancing and celebration everywhere. All the sufferings, all the difficulties, all the times of the cross and darkness are forgotten. After a while, however, it is noticed that there is something missing. Jesus cannot be found anywhere. He should be at the heart of the celebration! A group set off to find him and eventually he is found at the very edge of the crowd, staring into space. He seems to be waiting for something or someone. They ask him what he is doing, why he doesn't come and join the festivities. He gives a sigh and says, 'I want to wait here, I'm waiting for Judas.'

Love and forgiveness lie at the heart of the Gospel. That is what the vulnerable and crucified Christ tells us. This is the ultimate radical and revolutionary truth that has to be rediscovered. There is no other answer to the current hatred, fear and violence not only in Ireland but throughout the world. He sets before us the way of life and the way of death and calls on us to choose – choose life that we may live.

'For what seems to be God's foolishness is wiser than human wisdom, and what seems to be God's weakness is stronger than human strength.'

Lord, make us a channel for your peace.

# Acknowledgements

*Chapter 2.*
F.S.L. Lyons, *Culture and Anarchy in Ireland 1890–1939* (Oxford University Press 1979)

*Chapter 3.*
Lines from Stephen Spender's poem 'What I expected was' in *Selected Poems* (Faber and Faber 1965)

*Chapter 5.*
Lines from Siegfried Sassoon's poem 'Everyone Sang' in *Selections from Modern Poets* by J.C. Squire (Martin Secker 1921)
Quotations of George MacLeod taken from *Daily Readings with George MacLeod* edited by Ron Ferguson (Fount 1991)

*Chapter 6.*
Alf McCreary's book *Corrymeela – the Search for Peace* was helpful in the last part of this chapter
Janet Shepperson's poem was published in the collection called *Trio 5* (Blackstaff Press 1987)

*Chapter 7.*
Alf McCreary was again helpful in this chapter
Passage from Dervla Murphy's *A Place Apart* (John Murray Publisher)

*Chapter 9.*
Lines from 'Lord of the Dance' by Sydney Carter
Quotation from *A Matter of Life and Death* by John V. Taylor. I have also found his *The Go-Between God* most helpful in writing this book. Both are published by the SCM Press
Quote from a paper 'Christian Communities Today' given by John Harvey, Leader of the Iona Community, at a Corrymeela meeting in Portrush on 13th June 1992

*Chapter 10.*
Lines from a poem 'The Belfast Teenager 1974' in *The Wearing of the Black* (Blackstaff Press)

*Chapter 11.*
Lines from James Young's monologue 'Wee Davy', with permission from Emerald Records Limited, Templepatrick, Co. Antrim

*Chapter 12.*
Professor John White, *Interpreting Northern Ireland* (Clarendon Press)

*Chapter 13.*
Quotation from Bishop John Baker's book *The Foolishness of God*
The Faith and Politics book *Living the Kingdom* was useful in this chapter
The Judas story is from Tomás Ó Caoimh's book *Beginning to Pray* (Columba Press)

Further information about Corrymeela is available from:

The Leader,
Corrymeela Community,
Corrymeela House,
8 Upper Crescent,
Belfast BT7 1NT.
or:
Mrs Shirley Tasker,
Corrymeela Link Office,
P.O. Box 118,
Reading RG1 1CL.